BARBARA SCHERER
R.2 BOX 202 M 140
WATERVLIET, MI. 49098
PH. 463-8308

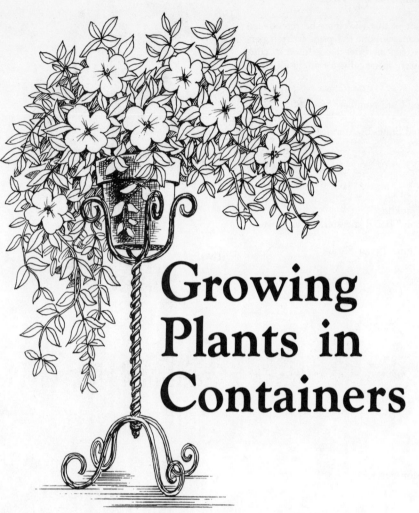

Growing Plants in Containers

Fred Bonnie
Garden Editor, *Southern Living Books*

Oxmoor House, Inc.
Birmingham

Copyright © 1976 by Oxmoor House, Inc.
Book Division of The Progressive Farmer Company
P.O. Box 2463, Birmingham, Alabama 35202

All rights reserved. No part of this book may be reproduced in any form or by any means without the prior written permission of the Publisher, excepting brief quotes used in connection with reviews written specifically for inclusion in a magazine or newspaper.

Library of Congress Catalog Card Number: 76–9280
ISBN: 0–8487–0440–1
Manufactured in the United States of America

First Printing 1976

Growing Plants in Containers

Editor: Candace Conard Franklin
Photography: Jack Goodson, Bob Lancaster, Louis Joyner,
  Fred Bonnie
Illustrations: Ralph Mark, June Taylor Shrum

Advisory panel:

John Floyd
Professor of Horticulture
Jefferson State College
Birmingham, Alabama

Fred C. Galle
Director of Horticulture
Callaway Gardens
Pine Mountain, Georgia

Dwight Hall
Extension Horticulturist
Texas Cooperative Extension Service
Overton, Texas

Ronald L. Shumack
Ornamental Horticulturist
Alabama Cooperative Extension Service
Auburn, Alabama

Contents

Introduction

Many small to medium-size plants can be grown in containers. Terrariums, bottle gardens, house plants, hanging baskets, and potted trees and shrubs are all examples of container gardens. In addition to these, ferns, palms, annual and perennial flowers, vegetables, herbs, and other groups of plants are well suited to growing in containers. For many Americans, growing plants in containers almost makes more sense than growing them in the open ground. Apartment dwellers have long appreciated the advantages of container gardening, but an increasing number of homeowners, especially those with small properties, are realizing that plants growing in containers not only require less room, but the plants can also be moved freely in the outdoor landscape to keep small areas of the garden lively and changing.

Depending on the plants you choose, container gardens can be suited to indoors or out. The selection of plants you may grow in container gardens is considerably broad since tender tropicals and subtropicals can be brought indoors during the winter. Plant selection is broadened further by virtue of the fact that soil for the container garden may be mixed and altered to achieve the right soil for plants whose soil requirements are exacting.

The decorative potential of container gardening is twofold: plants are a source of beauty and pleasure and so, too, are the containers. This does not mean that only the most elaborate, expensive containers are attractive. Often, old buckets, boxes, jars, and other "treasures" gleaned from the attic or basement make striking containers.

Growing Plants in Containers furnishes the beginning gardener with the information necessary to assure a successful initiation to the world of container gardening. The book also provides the more experienced gardener with new ideas. Extensive charts of plants adapted to container culture are included for information at a glance. Included also are a number of how-to photographs and line drawings, a glossary of garden terms to clarify unfamiliar words found in the text, and a fully cross-referenced index.

Plant Names

Both English and Latin names of plants are used throughout this book. The reason is simple: common, or English, names are impossible to standardize in a language which is spoken by over 300 million people who live in every corner of the world. Plant names may vary not only from country to country, but from state to state and even from county to county. Consequently, the only standardized name for most plants is the botanical, or Latin, name. Latin names are recognized not only by English speaking peoples, but throughout the Western world. Latin names do change from time to time when scientists and other researchers find reason to classify a plant with a different genus or if the plant becomes classified as a separate genus or species by itself. Our point in presenting the Latin names is not to suggest that you sit down and memorize them, but rather to allow you to identify plants correctly when purchasing plants or referring to horticultural encyclopedias. Jot down the names, Latin and English, of the plants you wish to purchase before going to a nursery or greenhouse. Then, if there is confusion about the English name, the plantsman will be able to tell from the Latin name precisely which plant you want.

Plant Hardiness Zone Map

The Plant Hardiness Zone Map is included to help you determine which plants are suited to the outdoor climate in your region of the country. Repeated references are made throughout this book to the zone numbers on the map. Locate your area on the map, take note of which growing zone you are in, and determine from the charts in Chapters 4 through 14 which plants may be left outside during the winter and which you should bring in before fall frost.

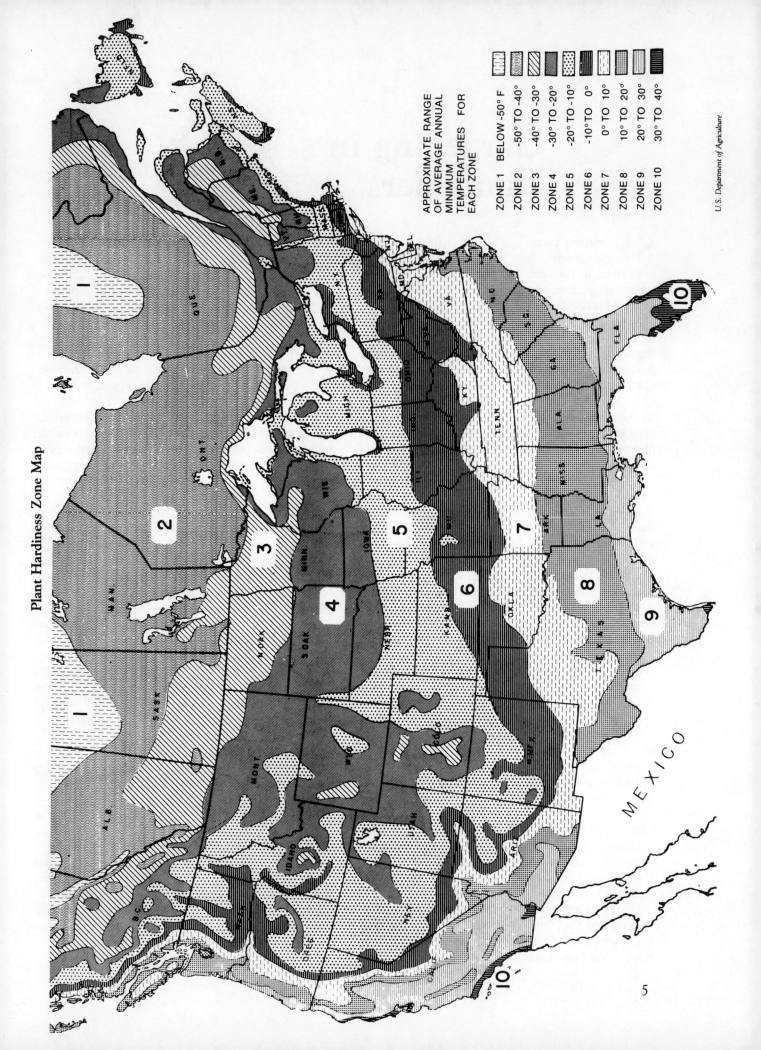

Plant Hardiness Zone Map

APPROXIMATE RANGE
OF AVERAGE ANNUAL
MINIMUM
TEMPERATURES FOR
EACH ZONE

ZONE 1 BELOW -50° F
ZONE 2 -50° TO -40°
ZONE 3 -40° TO -30°
ZONE 4 -30° TO -20°
ZONE 5 -20° TO -10°
ZONE 6 -10° TO 0°
ZONE 7 0° TO 10°
ZONE 8 10° TO 20°
ZONE 9 20° TO 30°
ZONE 10 30° TO 40°

U.S. Department of Agriculture

MEXICO

Gardening in Containers

Since earliest times, people have grown plants in containers where there was not room to grow them in the open ground. Today's urban and suburban gardeners are finding that container-grown plants offer great decorative potential, not only for indoors, but for outdoor living spaces as well. The selection of plants for container gardening is vast and includes plants from every major group of ornamental plants generally grown in the open ground. In addition, many vegetables and herbs can be grown successfully in containers.

The three essential elements of a container garden are the container, the soil mix, and the plants. All three are interdependent on one another.

Containers

In general, containers must be in proportion to the plants they contain. Select containers which will allow root growth. Do not use too large a container; the soil is liable to remain wet (as opposed to moist), thereby encouraging root rot and other potential problems. On the other hand, too small a container may cause the plant to become "pot-bound," forcing roots to grow around the soil ball or out the drainage holes in the bottom of the container. Most plants in this condition are unable to conduct moisture, nutrients, and oxygen properly and are therefore prone to problems. Some plants actually thrive in a pot-bound condition, but these are exceptions.

The height of the container should generally be about one-third to one-fourth the height of the plant in it. A certain measure of intuition will often best guide you in judging the appropriateness of container size.

Clay and plastic pots

Many plants grow satisfactorily in clay or plastic pots, the most commonly available containers. Pots are available in many sizes, from those with a diameter (at the top) of 2 inches to 2 feet.

Clay pots are more attractive than plastic containers, and they provide a healthier growing environment; but clay pots are also heavier, more fragile, and more expensive than the plastic. Plastic pots are often satisfactory for container gardens. Their lack of decorative appeal can be camouflaged in a number of ways, such as growing cascading plants which will conceal the container or placing the plants inside more interesting outer containers.

Care of plants in clay and plastic pots differs somewhat. Because clay is a porous material which allows rapid evaporation of soil moisture through the walls, plants in clay containers need to be watered more frequently than those in plastic or glazed containers. Clay pots can be beneficial, however, for plants that are sensitive to too much moisture. The more moisture-retentive plastic pots have the advantage of demanding less frequent watering.

Saucers

Place saucers under pots and other containers to catch excess moisture as it drains through the soil. Saucers can also be used as containers themselves for "dish gardens" of miniature cacti and succulents. Clay saucers are especially suited for dish gardens.

Saucers are necessary equipment for container gardening. Without saucers, excess water would

Select containers with specific plants in mind; consider plant size and rate of growth, drainage requirements, and where and how the plant is to be displayed.

drain through pots onto furniture, floors, and shelves.

Do not set saucers directly on floors or rugs; the dampness of the pot and saucer will cause staining. Place three or four small blocks of wood (½ to 1 inch thick) under the saucer before placing the pot on the floor. Not only does the slight elevation prevent stains, but it also permits air circulation under the saucer, encouraging evaporation of what dampness might collect there.

Wooden containers

The easiest containers to build are those made of wood. Tubs, planters, and boxes of all kinds can be suitable containers for plants. Window boxes are excellent for annual and perennial flowers and can be enjoyed from both inside the window and out. Small shallow boxes and drawers from old dressers make excellent seed flats.

The only serious disadvantage of wooden containers is their tendency to decay and eventually rot. Decay can be prevented, however, if the inside of the container is treated with a wood preservative before soil is added. Do not use creosote; it is toxic to plants. A reliable, nontoxic wood preservative is copper naphthenate.

The best materials from which to make wooden plant containers are redwood and cypress because they resist decay better than most other woods.

Tips for homemade containers

When making window boxes, use brass screws to hold the box together; nails may pull out if the wood becomes warped. Reinforce the inside cor-

Tips for Homemade Containers

Be sure the container has holes in or near the bottom to permit excess water to drain through.

Do not trust nails to hold hanging containers together; use only screws. The weight of the potting soil will soon pull nails apart.

Fasten blocks to the bottom of wooden tubs to assure the easy passage of excess moisture through the drainage holes in the bottom of the tub.

Staple fine-mesh hardware cloth against the inside of containers whose walls are not solid enough to hold potting soil in the container.

ners near the top with angle irons. Bore ½-inch drainage holes 6 inches apart along the bottom of the box. Put up strong braces for reliable support when mounting the box on a wall.

Wooden tubs and planters to be placed on patios, decks, porches, or balconies should rest on blocks or bricks for good support and to raise the box a few inches to allow good drainage and air circulation.

Ceramic containers

Ceramic containers are excellent for plants as long as drainage outlets are provided. Available in a wide range of sizes, ceramic containers often blend well with the decorating scheme of modern and contemporary homes. Because their glazed surfaces impede the escape of soil moisture through the walls, plants in ceramic containers require less watering, about the same amount as for plastic pots.

Ceramic containers, especially large ones, are more often used as jardinieres, rather than con-

tainers which hold the plant directly. The craftsmanship which goes into the making of good glazed pots is often extraordinary and fully deserving of the higher prices these containers command.

Jardinieres

Jardinieres are not containers for plants, but rather more decorative containers for already pot-

Place the plant in its original pot inside the jardiniere; then fill in around the first pot with pine bark nuggets to conceal the inner pot.

If the pot and jardiniere are nearly the same size, no filler material between the two is necessary. This bromeliad is an *Aechmea*.

An old bucket serves as a jardiniere for this schefflera (*Brassaia actinophylla*). A little imagination and a hunt through the attic or basement could turn up striking jardinieres for your plants.

ted plants. The less decorative container holding the plant is placed inside the jardiniere and the space between the two containers filled with pine bark nuggets, washed stones, sphagnum moss, or styrofoam packing "peanuts."

Jardinieres are not only quite lovely, they can also make watering plants in clay pots easier. Place a handful of gravel in the bottom of the jardiniere and spread it out so that the inner pot may be set on it. The gravel permits excess water from the inner pot to drain through easily rather than stand around the roots.

Planters

The term *planter* usually designates a large container. Planters may be stationary or movable. Stationary types, made of brick, railroad ties, or other materials, are often found along foundations, at entryways, or in other parts of the garden. Indoor stationary planters can add interest to a room by filling large, distractingly empty spaces. A long, narrow planter with hanging baskets suspended above it makes an effective room divider without robbing the room of its single room feeling. Unless the planter is quite stable, you will want to anchor it to the floor with angle irons and screws. Brick and stone or mortar planters should not require bolting.

Movable planters are useful if the plants growing in them require indoor protection during the winter or a change of location to adjust to the sun's changing path. The simplest way to assure movability is to install castors on the bottom of the planter.

Set plants in soil added directly to the movable planter, or set potted plants inside the movable planter and mulch with pine bark nuggets, washed stones, or the like to conceal the inner containers. The latter approach allows you to change the character of the plant material as frequently as you like.

Other containers

Containers other than pots, tubs, and planters are available everywhere. Old buckets, wagons, wheelbarrows, tea kettles, stumps, baskets, barrels, horse troughs, hollowed pieces of driftwood, sea shells, cement blocks, and any number of other attic or basement "finds" can be superb containers for plants. The container itself will often inspire the choice of plant to be grown in it. Squat, compact plants generally look good in squat, compact containers. Study the photographs throughout this book and note the relationships between plant forms and the shapes of their containers.

Shallow bowllike containers are excellent for growing bulbs, dish gardens of miniature cacti and succulents, and for bonsai trees.

Drill holes in the side of a barrel, fill the barrel with soil and plant slips of strawberries, ground ivy, babystears, artillery plant, or strawberry geranium in the holes and in the top.

Old livestock feeders are good containers for

A planter is simply a large container. Brick, stone, or railroad cross-tie planters are often built along foundations, walls, fences, and on patios and decks. Indoors, planters make interesting room dividers.

Mobility of containers is important when growing large, frost-tender plants such as this orange tree. A small dolley allows the gardener to bring the plant inside during the coldest part of the winter.

A pot rack can be used either indoors or out to economize on space while creating added interest in the plants themselves.

annual flowers or vegetables. Hollowed-out logs are good for flowers, too, especially wild flowers.

When matching plants and improvised containers, use annuals and short-lived perennials in containers which may rot or fall apart, and use more permanent containers for shrubs, house plants, ferns, and other more lasting plants.

Tools and Materials

In addition to containers, you will need the following tools and materials to begin a container garden:

> Packaged potting soil
> > *or*
> > Garden loam
> > Peat moss
> > Sphagnum moss
> > Sand
> > Perlite
> > Vermiculite
> Gravel
> Hardware cloth (for sifting soil)
> Watering can
> Misting bottle
> Spray bottle for pesticides
> Plastic 1-gallon jugs (3 or 4)
> Water-soluble fertilizer
> Trowel

The materials below are necessary for somewhat more specialized projects:

Seeds (for vegetables, herbs, cacti, annual flowers, some trees, shrubs, and vines)

Seed flats (for growing annual and perennial flowers, vegetables, and for propagating plants from cuttings)

Polyethylene or cellophane (for covering flats)

Hooks and hangers (for hanging baskets)

Pine bark nuggets (for trees, shrubs and double-potted plants)

Pruning shears (for grooming large house plants, trees, vines, and shrubs)

Rooting hormone (for propagating plants from cuttings)

Soils and Growing Media

Potting media range from simple garden loam to complex and exotic formulations of chemical and organic components, such as ground fir bark and elephant manure. Needless to say, the simpler the soil mixture, the easier to make or buy it. Many plants grow perfectly well in garden loam, and more than a few plants grow well in nothing more than a jar of water.

Potting soils

There are essentially three basic soil mixes for container gardens: loamy soil, sandy soil, and peaty soil. Loamy soil is mainly garden loam with peat moss and sand (or perlite) added. Sandy soil also contains peat moss and loam, but the preponderant component is sand. Peaty soils, in addition to sand and loam, contain high concentrations of organic matter such as peat moss, leaf mold, ground fir bark, cottonseed meal, compost, rotted sawdust, or dehydrated manure. Whatever type of soil you use, it should be sterilized first. Packaged mixes are already sterilized. Homemade mixes can be sterilized in your kitchen oven.

Loamy soil is sufficient for the vast majority of plants. To make 1 gallon of loamy potting soil, mix thoroughly:

1 quart loam
2 quarts peat moss, compost, or sawdust
1 quart sand
1 tablespoon 0–10–10 or equivalent low-nitrogen fertilizer
1 tablespoon dolomitic limestone

Sandy soil, which allows rapid drainage and evaporation of moisture, will be necessary for plants such as cacti, succulents, and other plants whose roots cannot tolerate soggy soil. To the basic loamy mix, add 1 to 2 quarts of sand or per-

How to Sterilize Potting Soil

For most plants, a soil mix of equal parts loam, sand, and peat moss is recommended. Perlite may be substituted for sand. Leaf mold or compost may be used in place of peat moss. Mix the components together and strain the soil mix through hardware cloth to obtain a fine texture.

Place strained soil mix in a plastic baking bag to minimize the odor of the cooking soil. Puncture the bag in a few places to allow air to escape. Place the soil-filled bag in a disposable aluminum foil baking pan.

Place the pan in the oven and bake at 250° for ½ hour. Allow the soil to cool before potting plants in it.

lite, depending on the degree to which you want to increase the drainage capacity of the soil. Many plants requiring sandy soil will also benefit from a layer of activated charcoal in the bottom of the container. Charcoal absorbs moisture on contact.

Peaty soils are of varying composition. An extremely peaty mix for plants requiring acid soil consists of 2 parts sphagnum moss or peat moss to 1 part composted pine needles or leaf mold. Such a mix is suited to camellias, hydrangeas, azaleas, heathers, and other plants whose moisture and acidity needs are easily satisfied by the soils of the rainy and humid southeastern and northwestern states.

Omit the limestone in peaty mixes. Most ferns do well in a mixture of 1 part loam, 1 part peat moss, and 1 part ground pine bark. Palms do well in an essentially loamy mix which has been supplemented with cottonseed meal or composted manure.

Growing plants without soil

Many plants will grow in plain water or in an artificial soil mix of peat moss and perlite. Bulbs may be grown on a tray of pebbles and water. A large group of plants, called *epiphytes*, possess roots which are capable of extracting moisture and nutrients directly from the air and therefore require neither water nor soil. (See Chapter Eight, Bromeliads.)

Growing plants in water is called hydroponics, water-culture, tank farming, chemical gardening, and "soil-less" culture. Growing plants by such a method is generally the same as when using soil, except that the required plant nutrients are dissolved in water rather than in the soil. This is not quite as simple as it may sound, since at least 11 plant nutrients must be supplied in proper balance. Three of these, nitrogen, phosphorus, and potassium, are called primary elements because plants need more of them. Three of the nutrients are called secondary elements, calcium, magnesium, and sulfur. The remainder of the nutrients are called trace elements and these include iron, manganese, boron, and others. In some cases molybdenum in trace amounts may also be needed.

Because of widespread interest in hydroponics as a hobby, several "package mixtures" are now available. These mixtures contain all the plant nutrients needed and are sold either as soluble powders or as liquid concentrates to be diluted with water. These commercial mixtures make hydroponic culture of plants much simpler.

Artificial soil mixes

Several basic artificial soil mixes, referred to as peat-lite mixes, have been developed. These artificial soils offer the gardener several advantages: they have a known fertility value; they have already been sterilized to control diseases, insects, weeds, and nematodes. Peatlite mixes also have a high moisture-holding capacity, yet drain well.

These are available as commercial products under brand names such as Jiffy-Mix, Kys-Mix, Peat-Lite Mix, MetroMix, and ProMix, and can

Artificial Soil Mix		
	for 1 cubic yard	*for 2 bushels*
Shredded sphagnum peat moss	11 bushels	1 bushel
Horticultural vermiculite #2, 3, or 4	11 bushels	1 bushel
Ground limestone	5 pounds	10 T[1]
Superphosphate, 20%, powdered	2 pounds	5 T[1]
5-10-5 fertilizer	6 pounds	15 T[1]
Borax (11%B)	10 grams (1 level tablespoon)	Do not add
Iron (Chelated such as NaFe, 138, or 330)	25 grams (2 level tablespoons)	1 level teaspoon
Nonionic surfactant[2]	2 ounces	1 level teaspoon

[1]Level tablespoon amounts.
[2]Mixed with 10 to 20 gallons of water/cubic yard of mix; 1 gallon for 2-bushel amount.

be purchased from retail garden supply centers. Or you can mix your own using the Artificial Soil Mix formula.

Thorough mixing of the components is essential. Mixing and storing should be done under the cleanest conditions possible to keep the mixture sterile. All tools and containers and mixing areas should be washed with a disinfectant, such as household bleach, to help prevent contamination.

If the peat moss is very dry, mix in ½ gallon of warm water per bushel of medium-grade moss to keep the dust down and permit easier wetting and handling. If possible, add water to peat moss several hours before mixing with other ingredients so it will be uniformly damp.

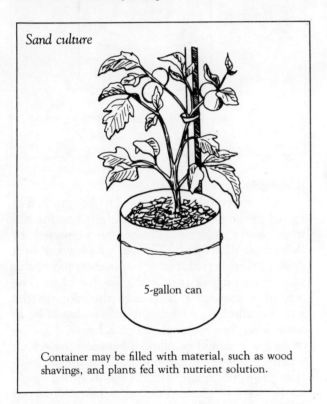

Sand culture

5-gallon can

Container may be filled with material, such as wood shavings, and plants fed with nutrient solution.

tom of the container or bed. Every few weeks water thoroughly with plain water to wash through any residual salts that may accumulate as a result of fertilizing.

Organic materials, such as sawdust and shavings, will use up part of the nutrients in the process of decay and will shrink or settle over a period of three or four months. At the end of the crop's growing season, the shrunken, decomposed material makes an excellent mulch for flower beds and shrubs.

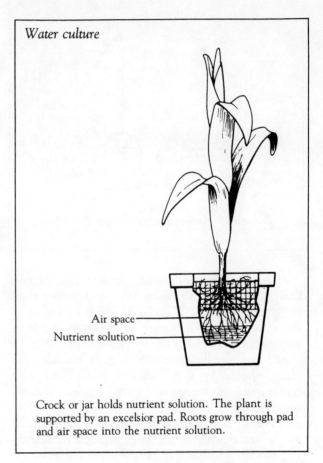

Water culture

Air space

Nutrient solution

Crock or jar holds nutrient solution. The plant is supported by an excelsior pad. Roots grow through pad and air space into the nutrient solution.

Sand culture

With this method, plants are grown in such materials as clean sand, sawdust, wood shavings cinders, brick screenings, perlite, vermiculite, peat moss, or haydite. Large flowerpots, 5-gallon cans, or raised benches make suitable containers and should have holes in the bottom to allow drainage.

Moisten the material with fertilizer solution and make repeated applications two or three times a week to keep it moist. Add enough solution each time to settle the material all the way to the bot-

Gravel culture

This is sometimes called the subirrigation method. Plants are set in a course, inorganic medium such as washed river gravel. Containers can be anything from flowerpots to shallow, waterproof beds made of concrete, wood, or metal. Metal containers should be treated to prevent corrosion.

Concrete and fiber glass beds are most commonly used by commercial hydroponic growers. The nutrient solution flows or is pumped into the bed until it is within an inch or so of the surface of the gravel. It is then pumped out or allowed to flow out by gravity into a reservoir or tank for reuse. Beds are flooded from one to five times a day, depending on seasonal temperature, size of plants, and texture of the gravel. The bed must be flooded often enough to prevent plants from wilting. A simple gravel-bed, home subirrigation unit is shown in the sketch.

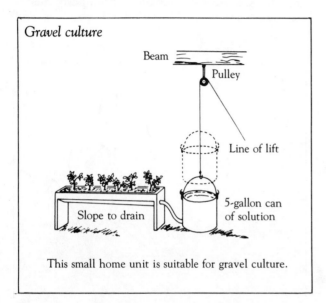

Gravel culture

Beam

Pulley

Line of lift

5-gallon can
of solution

Slope to drain

This small home unit is suitable for gravel culture.

A small, windowsill unit can be made of two flowerpots. One should be two sizes larger than the other, such as a 5- and a 7-inch pot, and be of the same shape. The larger one must be made of waterproof material such as plastic, ceramic, or glass. The smaller pot, which will contain the plant, should be a porous clay pot, filled with coarse sand or fine gravel. Using these two pots, construction is as follows:

- Prepare a collar made of plywood or a similar material with a hole large enough to accommodate the smaller pot. The collar rests on top of the larger pot.
- Pour the nutrient solution into the larger pot until the solution is level with the bottom of the smaller clay pot when sitting in place in the collar.
- Remove the smaller pot from the collar once or twice each day, and lower it into the larger pot. The solution will rise to the top of the gravel through the hole in the bottom.
- Lift out the smaller pot, place it back in the collar, and allow it to drain.

This method can be used for almost any small plant that is suited to container culture.

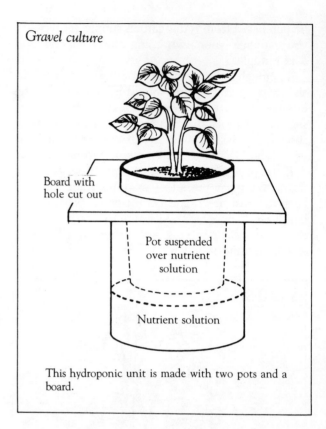

Gravel culture

Board with
hole cut out

Pot suspended
over nutrient
solution

Nutrient solution

This hydroponic unit is made with two pots and a board.

Water culture

For this method, plants must first be sprouted or rooted in sand or soil, then transferred to the nutrient water solution. Plants are supported by ¼-inch mesh screening, cloth, or plywood with drilled holes. It is also good to place on top of this support an inch or two of shavings or moss. The support is lowered to submerge the roots in the nutrient solution. At first the screen should be at water level, but as the plants grow larger, 2 inches of air space should be allowed between the screen and the surface of the solution. Tanks for the solution may be quart jars, large-mouthed jugs, earthenware or glass crocks, or waterproof tanks. Such tanks may be built of concrete, wood, or metal and coated with a pure grade of asphalt (not tar).

The biggest problem with water culture is aerating the water. Water does not retain enough free oxygen to supply plant roots, especially those of large plants. Therefore, a device to aerate water, such as the one used for bubbling air into small fish aquariums, is adequate for aerating a home hydroponic unit. Also, use of nutrients by the plant changes the concentration in the water, so the nutrient solution should be replaced or changed fairly often. Between changings, replace the solution as it is used by the plant so that the proper water level will be maintained.

Several house plants are adapted to simple water culture and will grow quite well in a jar containing 2 to 3 inches of water. Change the water weekly to prevent plants and water from becoming rancid. Add ¼ teaspoon of mild liquid fertilizer solution to the water every other time you change it. (See "Fertilizing," later in this chapter.) The following plants grow well with their roots immersed in water:

African evergreen	Devil's ivy
Chinese evergreen	English ivy
Coleus	Heartleaf philodendron
Cordyline,	Swedish ivy
Hawaiian ti	Wanderingjew

Lighting Needs

Some plants need more light than others. Many tropical plants, whose native habitat is the jungle, are accustomed to growing in the dense shade cast by giant trees. Other plants, such as cacti, are accustomed to the scorching sun. For purposes of discussion, four types of lighting situations are discussed for container gardens: direct sun, bright indirect or filtered sun, medium light, and low light.

Direct sun. Plants requiring direct sun should be placed where they will receive sunlight for at least 4 hours a day. Many flowering plants, such as chrysanthemum or geranium, require direct sunlight. Indoors, a window with a southern exposure is often in direct sun.

Bright indirect or filtered sun. Many plants need a bright, airy environment but will be scorched if placed in direct sunlight. Filtered shade is ideal for such plants on patios and outdoor areas. A room with southern exposure is usually bright enough, unless buildings are so close together that a considerable amount of light is lost. Direct sunlight filtered through a curtain also provides the right amount of light for plants that require bright indirect light.

Medium light. Most rooms in the home receive medium light. The more shaded areas of a well-lighted room may also have medium light. Many plants that require full light for optimum growth will adapt to medium light to sustain healthy but slower growth. Outdoor plants under the full umbrella of oaks and other dense shade trees receive medium light.

Low light. Rooms such as bathrooms and bedrooms usually receive the least amount of light in which plants are ordinarily kept. Although the dif-

ference in lighting may not seem significant to us, many plants have difficulty surviving in such subdued light. Happily, a surprising number of plants grow in low light, among which are cast-iron plant, Chinese evergreen, dieffenbachia, dracaena, philodendron, sansevieria, spathiphyllum, and maidenhair fern.

Natural light can also be supplemented by the use of artificial light.

Using artificial lighting

Most indoor plants can be grown successfully under ordinary fluorescent lamps. Specially designed, full-spectrum fluorescent lamps are also available, as are incandescent units. The most effective artificial lighting systems are a combination of fluorescent and incandescent lamps. In homes where exposure to natural sunlight is inadequate for most house plants, artificial lighting may solve

A lighted planter is useful for growing indoor plants where natural light is inadequate for good plant growth. These African violets are thriving under fluorescent lamps.

the problem. Plants grown under lamps receive a uniform amount of light over a longer period of the day (12 to 16 hours). Because the soil does not dry out as quickly under artificial light as opposed to natural lighting, plants require less frequent watering. The risk of scorching foliage is eliminated; most plants can be placed within 6 inches of fluorescent tubes or incandescent bulbs without being damaged.

Lamp fixtures may be mounted on a table or plant stand where plants are located, or you may prefer to build a planter with lamps mounted on it. One advantage of a planter is that pots can be concealed to give the planter a more natural look. Equip the planter with castors so that it can be moved to facilitate cleaning under and around it.

Whatever type planter you select, you can easily obtain lamps and mounting fixtures at any retail electrical supply house. Fixtures with white or silver backs will redirect and increase the light in the growing area. Place lamps so that light is directed toward the plants but not toward the room in which the planter is located.

If the glare emitted by fluorescent lamps is bothersome to you, another satisfactory lighting system consists of one 40-watt fluorescent lamp in combination with one 100-watt incandescent lamp.

Attach a 24-hour timer to the lamps rather than trying to remember to turn them off and on at the proper times. With a timer, you can be assured that plants are receiving the correct amount of light, even during vacations and other times when you will be away for more than just a day or two. Reduce lighting to about 10 hours a day when you are away. A slight reduction in light will also reduce water and fertilizer needs.

Two standard, 40-watt fluorescent lamps provide enough light for most foliage house plants; flowering plants may require more. Citrus, gardenia, geranium, gloxinia, and others will flower properly only with the use of high-output fluorescent lamps. Place plants with high light requirements within 6 to 12 inches of the lamps.

To measure light in a given location as precisely as possible, you may want to purchase a light meter at the garden supply store.

The standard measure of light is the *foot-candle*. A foot-candle is the amount of light cast by one candle on a surface 1 foot away.

Keep the surfaces of the lamps clean to assure maximum efficiency of the lighting system. After 18 to 24 months, depending on the amount of use, the lamps will need to be replaced. Replace them one at a time to allow a brief period of adjustment (100 to 150 hours) which fluorescent lamps require to reach peak efficiency. New lamps may perform erratically, so replacing them both at the same time could result in damage to the plants.

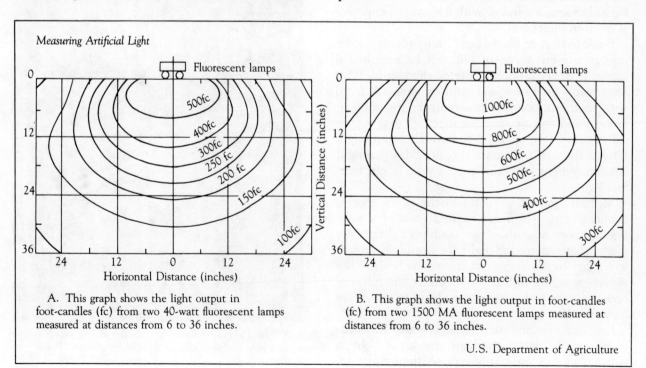

A. This graph shows the light output in foot-candles (fc) from two 40-watt fluorescent lamps measured at distances from 6 to 36 inches.

B. This graph shows the light output in foot-candles (fc) from two 1500 MA fluorescent lamps measured at distances from 6 to 36 inches.

U.S. Department of Agriculture

Places for Plants

Locations for container-grown plants must first satisfy the light, temperature, and moisture needs of the plants. Many bulbs, shrubs, ferns, and perennial flowers can be grown in container gardens on decks, patios, balconies, porches, terraces and in other prominent outdoor places.

House plants are called exactly that because they tolerate or require the warmth of the indoors during the cooler seasons. Many other plants, such as trees, shrubs, hardy ferns, woody vines, and bonsai trees require the cold of winter to break the dormancy (period of rest) they enter into at the end of the growing season. After sufficient cold treatment, flowering shrubs, potted bulbs, and dormant hardy ferns may be brought indoors in late winter and forced into bloom or into new leaf production in the case of ferns.

Weather permitting, move plants indoors or out when you are planning to entertain. Arrange the plants wherever they will be seen and enjoyed by your guests.

Indoor locations for container gardens

Place plants where they will receive the light they require for healthy growth. Plants receiving inadequate light develop spindly, elongated stems and pale leaves. No matter how nice the schefflera might look in the darkest corner of the bathroom, the schefflera requires bright, indirect light and will soon appear lusterless and droopy in a poorly lighted area.

Locate plants in the brightest light you can give them. Flowering plants generally require a lot of light, even direct sunlight, for 4 to 6 hours a day. Windowsills or shelves built inside window frames are good places for small to medium-small plants. Place large plants in low planters or on the floor. Dish gardens or terrariums can go on coffee tables, end tables, desks, telephone stands, and other unobtrusive places.

Avoid placing fragile plants near doors where they may be exposed to drafts and temperature fluctuations. Avoid, also, placing plants where they will be too near registers, radiators, and other sources of hot, dry air.

Some plants, such as ferns, spathiphyllum, cast-iron plant, Chinese evergreen, dracaena, dieffenbachia, and others can tolerate a relatively low level of light. (See charts at the end of Chapter Four for the light requirements of most common house plants.) Use low-light plants in low-light areas of your home, such as bedrooms and bathrooms.

Indoor plants as decoration

Decorating your home with plants is a good deal less expensive than decorating with framed artwork or antique furniture. Plants, in fact, are even more compatible with the restraint and "open space" of contemporary decorating schemes than with older trends in interior design. A single, large plant can fill a corner or relieve the dead expanse of a bare wall. Small plants are pleasing

Restraint in decorating with plants can effectively direct attention to the plants. The weeping fig featured here becomes the dominant factor in the decor of this room.

embellishments for dining tables, book shelves, breakfast bars, windowsills, night tables, dressers, bathroom counters, and any number of other areas which, despite their smallness, seem to need a plant.

Use plants individually or mass them in one or two key places in the room, but avoid scattering plants all over; most lose their distinctiveness if their placement causes too great a dispersal of visual attention.

The true plant enthusiast may want to fill every inch of free space with plants. The mass of plants rather than any individual plant here creates the decorating theme.

When massing plants together, be aware of the compatibility of plant textures at your disposal. Place large-leaved, coarse-textured plants together and fine, airy-topped, small-leaved plants together. Some good combinations are as follows:

Large plants, broad leaves
Saddleleaf philodendron, India-rubber tree, monstera, fiddleleaf fig, bearspaw fern, dieffenbachia, Japanese aralia, Chinese fan palm

Large plants, small leaves or leaflets
Weeping fig, schefflera, some crotons, false aralia, lace aralia, many palms

Medium-size plants, spadelike leaves
Spadeleaf philodendron, burgundy philodendron, caladium, African evergreen

Large straplike leaves
Corn plant, Hawaiian ti plant, some bromeliads, Chinese evergreen, cast-iron plant, screwpine

Slender straplike leaves
Spider plant (airplane plant), *Dracaena marginata*, yucca, Sander's dracaena, Christmas cactus, elephant-foot tree

Smooth, small variegated leaves
Variegated Swedish ivy, aluminum plant, wanderingjew, waxplant

Small to medium-size, hairy or wrinkled leaves
African violet, strawberry geranium, geranium, rex begonia, panamiga, piggyback plant, gloxinia, 'Emerald Ripple' peperomia, purple passion plant, fittonia

Smooth, fleshy, succulent leaves
Jade plant, *Peperomia*, snake plant (mother-in-law tongue), waxplant, plush plant (*Echeveria*), hen-and-chickens, moonstones, burn plant (*Aloe*)

Small plants, small leaves
Artillery plant, babystears, maidenhair fern, rosaryvine, bridalveil wanderingjew, asparagus fern

Brightly colored foliage
Coleus, crotons, poinsettia, prayer plant, copperleaf, caladium, Hawaiian ti plant, some bromeliads

Delicate foliage
Asparagus fern, false aralia, lace aralia

Large ferns
Boston fern, bearspaw fern, staghorn fern, occidental fern, tree fern (*Cibotium*), mother fern

Miniature indoor gardens
Terrariums, dish gardens, indoor bonsai, and other miniature gardens adapted to indoor conditions can fit comfortably in the decorating scheme of a room. A window filled with shelves of terrariums or a single small terrarium set unobtrusively at the end of a bookcase or record rack can add a pleasing, indoor, "keyhole garden" effect.

Coffee tables, dining tables, kitchen counters, and bathroom counters are all appropriate places for miniature gardens, especially enclosed miniature gardens.

Flowering miniatures, such as miniature roses, bulbs, and annuals, should be given the sunniest locations possible, as should miniature cactus gardens. Tropical and woodland terrariums, however, can often tolerate medium- to low-light conditions, depending on the plants selected.

A small "window greenhouse" is a superb home for plants, enhancing the decorative appeal of the home from both inside and out.

A shelf along the top of a fence or wall can be an excellent place to display potted plants.

Container gardens outdoors

The most trouble-free plants for outdoor containers are woody plants such as trees and shrubs. Bulbs such as tulips, daffodils, crocus, and others, depending on the winter temperatures in your area, are also undemanding plants for outdoor container gardens, as are hardy ferns.

Most bonsai trees require outdoor locations year-round and should not be brought indoors for more than a few hours at a time. Outdoor shelves are adequate display areas for bonsai specimens.

Container vegetable gardens must be grown outside during the warm season since the indoor environment is seldom light or humid enough to promote optimum growth.

During the summer, bring your indoor plants out for a season of fresh air. The increased humidity and air circulation will restore vigor to winter-tired house plants.

Hanging containers can be suspended from eaves, wall hangers, or other overhead structures which are strong enough to provide reliable support.

Do not locate containers where they will present a hazard to people. Bumping your head on a low-hanging, large wooden or metal hanging container can be quite painful.

Entries are more inviting when adorned with plants. Featured here are wax begonias and geraniums on the bench and a yucca in the large urn.

Decks and patios can be made more lively by adding container-grown plants

Imagine this patio without plants. The raised planter along the windows softens the lines where the glass meets the concrete, and the hanging baskets of Boston fern seem to lower the overhanging eaves. Plants in the foreground are saddleleaf philodendron and maidenhair fern.

Temperature and Humidity

Plants in containers outdoors seldom suffer from low humidity except in the most arid regions of the country. Indoor plants, however, often suffer from the high temperatures and low humidity present in most homes, especially during the winter. Moisture in house plant soil evaporates quickly both night and day, whereas moisture in the form of dew would tend to settle at night on outdoor plants. Compensation can be made for both the temperature and humidity conditions in our homes.

First, do not locate plants above radiators, registers, or other outlets for artificial heating. The direct flow of hot, dry air on the plants will cause their rapid demise.

Windows are ideal locations for many plants because they are cooler at night than other locations. A night temperature of 60° is good for most indoor plants. Before displaying plants in windows, however, be certain that the light conditions during the day are correct for those particular plants.

Humidity can be increased anywhere in a room by placing plants on a tray of pebbles or gravel and water. Fill the bottom of a shallow tray with 1 inch of gravel or pebbles, and fill the tray with water so that plant containers may be set on the

pebbles without being in contact with the water. Contact with the water will cause water to be drawn up through the drainage hole in the bottom of the container, keeping the soil too wet.

Locate plants above sinks to provide a humid environment for the plants and add interest to kitchens and bathrooms.

Watering and Misting

The greatest cause of container plant mortality is improper watering. Overwatering is more fatal than underwatering, but both can do considerable damage to plants. Symptoms of both extremes are similar—wilting and decline. Most plants can recover easily from minor wilting due to lack of water, but plants whose roots are left standing in water for a prolonged period cannot conduct oxygen through those roots to the rest of the plant. The suffocating effect on the plants is often fatal.

The first rule in caring for container-grown plants is not to overwater. Learn to gauge the moisture content of the soil by its color and feel. Generally, the drier the soil, the lighter its color. If moisture is not added, the soil surface becomes cracked and tends to pull away from the sides of the container. At this stage or before, wilting occurs. Water plants before they wilt. When the soil is dry enough to crumble between your fingers, apply water.

Some plants require more water than others. Soil for spathiphyllum and most ferns, for ex-

Raise humidity around indoor plants with a pebble tray. Nearly any shallow container, such as this old skillet, can serve as the tray. Place gravel or small stones in the tray, place the plant on the gravel, and fill the tray with water to the top of the gravel but not high enough to touch the pot. Humidity is increased slightly by the evaporating water. Refill to the correct level every few days.

A watering can is the best device for watering container-grown plants. Plants here are (top to bottom) asparagus fern, Swedish ivy, and coleus.

ample, should be kept somewhat moist all the time. Flowering plants generally require more water than foliage plants, especially during the growing season, but even with these, do not overwater.

A number of factors can affect the moisture needs of plants. Evaporation is more rapid in a warm, dry room than in a cool room or on a shady patio. The potting soil also makes a difference; some potting media retain moisture due to the addition of peat or sphagnum moss, whereas sandy potting soils allow water to drain through more quickly. The type of container used also influences the frequency of watering. Clay containers absorb a great deal of moisture and permit rapid evaporation; plastic, ceramic, or metal containers retain moisture without absorbing it. Water plants in plastic containers only half as frequently as those in clay or porous containers.

Double potting

Overwatering is less likely to occur if plants are double potted. This method provides moisture for the plant through the sides of the pot. Only po-

rous pots, such as those made from clay or peat, should be double potted. Plastic, metal, or ceramic containers cannot be double potted because these materials do not allow the passage of moisture and air.

After potting the plant in a clay pot, set the pot inside a large, watertight container and fill the space between the containers with sphagnum moss. Raise the height of the inner pot, if necessary, by putting coarse gravel in the bottom of the outside container. Water the soil inside the clay pot and the moss outside it. As the plant needs moisture, it can draw water through the walls of the clay pot. Keep the moss slightly moist all the time. Double potting also retards moisture evaporation through the sides of an exposed pot.

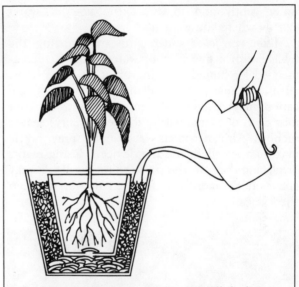

Double potting makes watering easier. Fill the bottom of a large pot with pebbles or broken pottery. Place the pot containing the plant inside the larger pot and fill in around it with sphagnum moss. Keep the moss moist. Water applied to the moss will seep through the sides of clay pots and keep the soil around the roots evenly moist.

Double potting is especially helpful with plants requiring high humidity or with plants growing in dim light. Because the soil dries slowly, frequent watering is not as critical as it is when plants are grown in pots exposed to air.

Do not allow pots to stand in water. The excess salts which the water has washed through will be reabsorbed by the soil and will cause root damage.

Do not apply excessively warm or cold water to plants. Water should be room temperature or lukewarm. Tap water is fine for house plants in most sections of the United States. In cities where the water contains a great deal of chlorine, the water should be allowed to sit overnight in an uncovered container before being applied to plants. This allows some of the chlorine to evaporate. Water from water softeners should not be used at all.

The most common method of watering is watering from the top of the pot. The water then seeps down into the root zone. When watering by this method, keep the flow of water gentle to avoid washing soil away from roots and to avoid splashing water onto the leaves. Water splashed onto foliage often encourages the spread of diseases. A watering can is the best device for watering indoor plants. The long spout of the can allows you to water gently and to direct the flow of water exactly where you want it.

Misting or *foliar watering* means spraying the foliage with a fine mist of water. This is recommended for humidity-loving plants such as ferns, citrus, and many others. Plants in a warm, dry location may require light misting daily. Do not mist cacti or plants with pubescent (hairy) leaves such as African violets. A simple spray bottle makes an excellent misting device. Hosing plants or placing them in the shower under a light spray about once a month is an excellent way to clean the foliage.

Misting the leaves of plants every few days raises humidity and simulates the rainfall to which plants are accustomed in their natural environment. Do not mist cacti, however, or plants with hairy leaves, such as those of African violet.

How much water how often?

Most container plants fall roughly into three watering categories: plants which require frequent watering, plants which require medium watering, and plants which require light watering. The first group should be kept fairly moist (but not soaked) all the time. Plants that require a medium amount of water should be watered about once a week. Water the plants slowly until water drains from the bottom of the container. Allow the soil to absorb it gradually; then allow the soil to become moderately dry before watering again. Most plants can be watered in this manner. Low-moisture plants, such as cacti and succulents, should receive nearly as much water per application as medium-moisture plants, but apply the water less frequently. For cacti, too much water means certain death.

During the winter, water plants less frequently. This is a period of rest for most plants during which they are particularly susceptible to damage resulting from overwatering. Cacti and other succulents should be watered only enough to keep them from shriveling.

However, high room temperatures do encourage the loss of moisture through evaporation. Each winter, many house plants die in hot, arid homes. For this reason, double potting and misting are especially recommended for plants whose moisture and humidity requirements are high.

Potting and Repotting

Container-grown plants must be repotted when their roots become restricted and matted on the outside of the soil ball. Some plants require repotting more frequently than others. In general, fast-growing plants may need to be repotted twice a year. Most plants require repotting only once a year and some do not need repotting for two or three years.

A number of flowering plants, such as African violet, geranium, and begonia, grow best when they are slightly pot-bound (have crowded roots), but these are the exception.

The best time to repot overcrowded plants is in the spring as new growth begins. However, many plants can be safely repotted at any time of the year. Do not wait until spring to repot severely crowded plants; they may die from root strangulation before spring arrives.

Check plants whose roots you suspect may be crowded. If plants wilt quickly between waterings, and growth is generally slow and stunted, repotting may be necessary. If roots begin to protrude through the drainage hole in the bottom of the pot or appear on the surface of the soil, the plant needs to be repotted. The surest method of finding

A simple potting bench makes potting and repotting easier and more enjoyable. A large, shallow box and four cement blocks are all you'll need to eliminate bending over to work with the plants.

out is to remove the plant from the pot to inspect the root ball. In the case of small plants, moisten the soil slightly to make it cohere, then tip the pot upside down to slide the plant out. If it does not come out readily, tap the side of the pot gently. If the roots are matted around the outside of the soil ball, the plant must be repotted.

To remove a large plant from its container, lay the container on its side, and gently tap the container off the root ball with a block of wood and a hammer. Do not pull the plant out by the stem.

After removing the plant from its pot, carefully loosen the larger roots that are matted, but do not crumble the soil ball. Remove any roots that have rotted.

Repotting does not always mean transferring the plant to a larger container. Mature plants that might become difficult to handle if allowed to grow any larger should have their roots pruned and be repotted in the same size container. Cut back the top growth to maintain a balance between roots and top. If roots are cut, but the amount of top growth the roots must support is not, the roots will have difficulty recovering from the shock of being pruned and repotted. For young plants, however, select a container at least 2 inches larger in diameter; then cover the drainage

hole with a small piece of crockery from a broken pot. Fill the bottom of the pot with 1 inch of pebbles or gravel to assure good drainage.

Add enough potting soil so that the top of the root ball, when placed in the pot, will be about ½ inch below the rim of the pot. Fill in around the sides of the root ball with potting soil, and firm it with a tamping stick. Water the new soil gently to settle it; then add more soil as needed to bring the level of the soil up to the top of the root ball. Do not fill the pot to the rim; water and soil will wash over the sides when you are watering the plants.

Many plants, such as ferns, should be divided at the roots to form new plants. Repotting time is a good time to do this.

Very large plants are often troublesome to repot. Trees, shrubs, and other plants large enough to require tubs can be kept in the same container

Repotting Plants

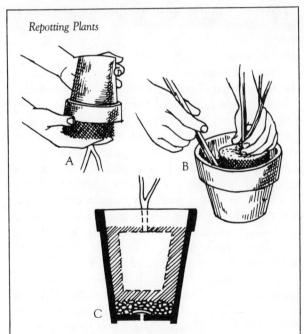

A. Moisten soil, then turn pot upside down to remove the plant. If it does not slide right out, gently tap the side of the pot. Trim excess growth off roots severely matted around the root ball.

B. Fill the bottom of the new pot with pebbles or 1-in gravel. Add 1 inch of potting soil and set the plant in the pot. Adjust soil underneath until the top of the root ball is 1 inch lower than the rim of the pot. Fill in around the root ball with soil, tamping it gently in place with a small stick. Water the plant to settle the soil.

C. A side view of the potted plant. If repotting is done because the plant is root-bound, select a new pot at least 2 inches larger in diameter than the old one.

for several years if they are topdressed. Topdressing consists of removing the upper 2 inches of soil, including roots, and replacing it with fresh potting soil.

Potting new plants

Plants purchased from mail-order houses or cuttings you have rooted must be potted as soon as possible. Select a container with good drainage. Do not cramp the roots together. They should be spread out as much as possible to encourage rapid, untraumatic establishment. If the roots reach the walls of the container, the container is too small. Potting plants in too small a container hampers their development, and they will also need to be repotted sooner. Fill the container with soil to 1 inch below the rim; firm it, and water thoroughly.

Fertilizing

Fertilizer supplies nutrients that are essential to plant growth. Plants must have nitrogen, phosphorus, and potassium, as well as a number of other elements to sustain life.

There are essentially two approaches to feeding plants: frequent, light fertilization with a standard formulation or occasional fertilization (once every 3 or 4 months) with a slow-release fertilizer. Frequent, light fertilization results in vigorous plants whereas feeding at greater intervals results in slower growing plants that require less water, less light, and less frequent grooming and repotting. Fast growing plants generally require more attention than those whose rate of growth is slower.

There is, of course, something to be said for both fertilizing methods, depending on just how much time you have to spend with your plants.

Newly purchased plants have very likely been fertilized recently and should need no fertilizer for at least 1 to 2 months. Be careful not to overfertilize container plants. The tiny hair roots of plants may be severely damaged by concentrations of fertilizer in the soil. Furthermore, the rapid growth stimulated by overfertilizing is often spindly and weak.

Do not fertilize plants during the winter months; this is a period of rest in the annual cycle of many plants. Exceptions to this rule include plants that bloom in the winter or that bloom year round, but even with these plants reduce the fertilizer dosage between November and February.

Liquid fertilizers, available at garden supply centers, are the easiest to use and to store. You can also concoct a liquid fertilizer solution at home by adding 1½ teaspoons of concentrated, water-soluble fertilizer, such as 20-20-20, to 1 gallon of water. Fertilizer for liquid solutions must be soluble in water; that is, able to dissolve in water. Apply the solution at the rate of ¼ cup to a 6-inch plant pot, ½ cup to an 8-inch pot, and 1 cup to a 10-inch pot. Household ammonia is an effective fertilizer for most foliage plants. Dissolve 1 teaspoon of ammonia in 1 quart of water, and apply the solution at the rate of ½ cup to a 6-inch pot. Fish emulsion is also a recommended fertilizer and is available commercially. Both, however, have strong odors.

As with all garden chemicals, keep fertilizer out of the reach of children and pets.

Apply mild solutions of fertilizer once every 2 to 4 weeks. The more frequent the feeding, the weaker the dosage should be.

To promote slower growth, especially for large plants, fertilize once every 3 to 6 months, depending on the plant. Slow-release fertilizers are available at garden supply centers. The best approach to fertilizing plants on a low maintenance schedule is to feed them only when they show signs of a need for fertilizer.

Common symptoms of nutrient deficiency in plants include yellowing of leaves, a general dullness of color, and perhaps even the loss of some leaves. However, if plants exhibit these symptoms, be sure that under-fertilization is the problem before adding more fertilizer. Overwatered plants, or plants whose roots have become pot-bound, may also exhibit these signs. Check the root ball for moistness and for excessive root growth around the outside of the soft ball. When you do add fertilizer, do so with care, applying it in small doses until you are satisfied that the plant did, in fact, need feeding. Applying unneeded fertilizer to a plant whose health is poor will almost surely worsen the situation.

If fertilizer begins to accumulate and to form a white residue on the surface of the soil, gently scrape it off and replace whatever soil you have removed with fresh potting soil. Water thoroughly from the top of the pot to wash salts and excess fertilizer out of the soil. Plants that are watered by immersion or by subirrigation are especially prone to such surface accumulations of fertilizer.

Grooming

A few routine practices will keep your plants looking their best. The leaves of most smooth-leaved plants should be wiped with a wet sponge or cloth from time to time to remove accumulations of dust and to maintain the glossy appearance of such plants as schefflera, rubber plant, dracaena, dieffenbachia, and other broadleaf, smooth foliage plants. Do not wash plants with pubescent (hairy) foliage, and do not remove the powdery coating on leaves of succulents such as echeveria or kalanchoe. Plants with pubescent foliage may be brushed lightly, however, to remove dust and other grime that may accumulate. Use a soft brush, such as a baby's hairbrush. Handle foliage carefully when cleaning it.

Plants whose stems have become elongated with sparse growth should be cut back to maintain a uniform appearance. If growth is sparse along the entire stem, pinch it off at its junction with the main stem or at soil level if the leggy stem emanates directly from the root system. If growth is

Clean smooth-leaved plants with a damp sponge and soapy water to remove dust and grime and to eliminate small populations of insects.

When white salts, mold, and other grime collect on clay pots, scrub them with a stiff-haired brush. Scrape the soil surface gently with an old spoon to remove any salts which may have collected there. Salts in contact with roots can impair plant growth. Water thoroughly to wash remaining salts through the soil.

sparse only along a section of stem that protrudes beyond the rest of the plant, pinch it back enough to eliminate the protrusion.

Remove withered foliage. It is not uncommon for a few old leaves to die now and then; plants are not immortal.

Faded flowers should be removed as soon as they are spent. Otherwise, the flowers will produce seed. If the plant is not allowed to mature its seed, it will continue to produce flowers in its attempt to produce seed. If too many seeds are allowed to mature, the plant has completed its need to produce flowers. Many flowers will then die. Pinching off faded flowers can also stimulate branching and bud formation, producing a bushier plant with more flowers.

Give all your plants a half turn every 2 or 3 weeks. The side of the plant which receives more light is generally a little perkier than the darker side. This is especially true of plants that are in windows. Turning plants periodically to distribute light evenly gives them a uniform and healthy appearance.

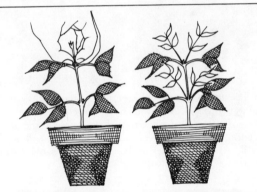

To make sparse plants bushier, pinch off the tips of stems. Long, ungainly stems can also be pinched back to maintain an appearance of even growth. New shoots will arise where the old stems were pinched. Do not throw the pinched parts away; they can be rooted to form new plants.

Summer and Vacation Care

Locate most of your plants outdoors during the summer. The fresh air and increased humidity alone will do your plants more good than the pampering you might bestow on them indoors. For haggard, winter-weary plants, being repotted in fresh soil and brought outdoors will work wonders.

Patios, porches, decks, and other outdoor living areas are good places for plants. Many gardeners who have outdoor garden space prefer to dig holes in the garden and bury plants up to the rims of their pots. Plants which are "plunged" into the garden in this manner are better able to retain soil moisture between waterings because evaporation is retarded. In areas of average rainfall, plunged plants may need no manual watering during the summer.

During vacations, plunge plants in the garden or ask a friend or neighbor to water your plants for you. Plants in hanging baskets may need water every day, depending on their exposure to the sun. If there is no one on whom you can call to water your plants, double-pot those plants which require the most watering. Move plants into the shade wherever possible to reduce the rate of

Wick system watering will keep plants sufficiently watered for up to two weeks. Water in the sink is conducted along sections of cotton clothesline rope. Poke a hole in the soil in each pot to insert one end of the wick. Firm the soil around the wick. Anchor the wick in the water with a saucer. Water plants thoroughly to start the siphon action.

Medium-size, mature plants in large pots dry out more slowly than those in small pots. When the gardener must be away for several days, he can provide adequate moisture and humidity for his plants by making a shelf in the bathtub with two bricks and a board, setting the plants on the shelf, then filling the tub with water to the level of the board. Water the plants thoroughly before leaving.

evaporation of soil moisture. Another method is to move plants into showers, bathtubs or sinks filled with a few inches of water. Support plants on blocks or empty pots just above the water.

One more method of providing for plants while you are vacationing is to drench the plants thoroughly; then place them in ordinary plastic bags available at the grocery store. Secure the bag around the pot, and fasten it at the base of the stem to reduce moisture evaporation. Move bagged plants to a shady area.

As cool fall weather approaches, move plants back indoors; do not wait until frost arrives, because you may forget one or two. Most house plants are from the tropics and may suffer minor damage at temperatures well above frost, especially if the drop is sudden and follows rather high temperatures.

Inspect plants for insects or signs of fungus diseases before placing them indoors with your other plants. Keep plants with problems, even small problems, segregated until you can treat them. (See Chapter Fifteen, Problems in Container Gardens.)

Moving container-grown plants long distances

If you must relocate to a new home in another city or state, the care you exercise in preparing your plants for the move will determine their ability to survive.

Water the plants thoroughly; then cover them with plastic bags to retain as much moisture as possible. Small plants can be covered with sandwich bags or cellophane. Cover large plants with bags such as those used to cover dry-cleaned garments. Large, sprawling plants, such as saddleleaf philodendron (*P. selloum*), will require particular care. Gather the stems together in an upright position, and secure them by looping a strip of soft cloth around them; then cover the plant with a dry cleaning bag. Plants in hanging containers should be covered with plastic and, if possible, situated in the moving vehicle where they can hang. Secure all plastic covering below the rim of the pot to assure moisture retention.

Most plants can survive without light for 2 or 3 days if they have adequate moisture. Beyond 3 days, however, recovery from the trip becomes increasingly difficult. If it is at all possible, transport plants in a car or other vehicle in which they may receive light. If plants must be moved in a closed vehicle, check them each day of the trip. Avoid extreme temperatures, either too hot or too cold.

Hanging Gardens

Perhaps the most exciting way of displaying container-grown plants is to pot them in baskets and hang the baskets from overhead or wall bracket supports. Hanging gardens have a special importance for today's metropolitan or suburban gardener, whose space for growing plants may be limited. Hanging gardens can be single baskets or pots, or if you have very solid beams which are easy to locate, containers can be suspended one below the other to create a multilevel hanging garden. Retail garden supply centers stock containers and hangers to suit any taste.

Hanging baskets can be hung inside or outside, wherever you can provide solid support for the hangers and wherever the plant will not be in the way. During spring and summer, hang plants outside on patios, decks, balconies, and other outdoor living spaces. Indoors, plants are commonly hung in windows, in empty corners of rooms, or against walls as a refreshing alternative to mirrors, framed paintings, and posters. Plants suspended over kitchen sinks receive the added benefit of increased humidity. Special precautions must be taken, however, to avoid damage from water dripping from the hanging baskets.

Locations for hanging gardens must ultimately depend on the light, temperature, and humidity requirements of the plants you wish to hang. The

Hanging baskets are suited to both indoor and outdoor locations.

A sunny window is the best location for indoor hanging baskets. The plant featured here is a spider plant, also called airplane plant.

27

chances are excellent, however, that there is a plant adapted to nearly any location you may choose, both indoors and out.

An infinite variety of containers can be used as hanging baskets. Commercially available containers are usually designed from galvanized wire, plastic, terra cotta, ceramic, or wood. Select containers that do not lose moisture rapidly. Solid plastic or wooden containers are preferred; clay pots require twice as much watering because moisture evaporates rapidly from them.

It is not difficult to make an attractive hanging basket that retains moisture. Choose a wire basket and line it generously with either coarse sphagnum moss or sheet moss. Wet the moss prior to lining the basket. Plastic and papier-mâché liners are also available for this purpose. Next, cut a layer of polyethylene plastic to fit inside the moss lining and fill the plastic liner with potting soil mix. To assure proper drainage, punch holes through the plastic in the bottom of the basket. Add potting soil to the desired level and set the plants.

Because of evaporation problems, hanging baskets are usually more successful when located in the shade and not exposed to hot sun. Plants of drooping or trailing habit are most appropriate for such containers, since hanging baskets display their flowers and foliage to best advantage.

The most important single aspect of growing plants in hanging baskets is to use a proper soil medium. It should be loamy in texture, drain well, and hold necessary moisture for the plants.

A good potting mix to use in hanging baskets is a combination of about two-thirds organic material (peat moss, compost, bark, etc.) and one-third soil, sand, or perlite. These proportions should be adequate for proper drainage and for ample air circulation to the root system.

Once the soil is properly mixed and a small amount of slow-release fertilizer is added, the basket is ready to be planted. Set each plant firmly in place, no deeper in the potting soil than it was previously growing. After planting, thoroughly soak the entire basket in a tub of water; then hang the basket in its intended location.

Supports

Do not trust nails, no matter how large they are, to hold heavy baskets or clay containers. Not only are nails undependable, but the larger the nail, the worse it looks. Hook and eye screws will hold more weight and are often available in decorative designs. If you buy an eye screw and your hanger also has a loop at the end, you'll need to purchase an **S** hook (shaped like the letter S) to connect them.

Most ceilings are made of gypsum board or plaster over lath. Hook and eye screws will easily pull out of these ceilings with the weight of the basket. Locate a beam in the ceiling (*beams*, also called *joists*, are heavy boards, usually 2 x 6s or 2 x 8s, against which the ceiling is mounted) by tapping with your knuckles along the ceiling until the sound becomes less hollow and you feel something solid behind the gypsum board or plaster. Beams are spaced as close together as 16 inches or as far apart as 24 inches, and sometimes farther. Determine the direction one beam runs in order to determine the pattern of all the support beams; then determine if the location of beams affects your choice of locations for the basket.

Once you have settled on a place to hang the basket, taking into account light exposure, dripping, humidity, and exposure to drafts as well as location of beams, drill a pilot hole and screw in the eye or hook until you can no longer see the threads in the screw.

False ceilings usually have no wooden joists. If this is the case in your home, use wall brackets. Baskets which are half-round are available for wall hangers; single hanging containers may be mounted on them. Or purchase racks in which to set two or more small pots.

Walls, like ceilings, are made of soft materials that will not support the weight of a potted plant. The outer materials are mounted on a series of vertical beamlike structures called *studs*. Tap on the wall with your knuckles until you locate a stud. Wall studs are usually spaced about 16 inches apart. When you locate a wall stud that is in a convenient place to hang plants, drill a pilot hole and screw in the wall mounts and brackets.

Hangers

Most hanging containers are sold with hangers, but you may wish to hang a container you already have. You can buy hangers at the garden supply store, or you can make them yourself out of a number of materials.

Hangers either attach to the rim of the container or they loop under it and cradle it. The variety of hangers is nearly as vast as that of containers. Wire, chain, rope, plastic, macrame, leather, and braided fabric are all materials that can be used to make hangers. Rim hangers are best made from wire, chain, and plastic, whereas cradle hangers are made from more supple materials.

Be certain that whatever material you choose or whatever type of hanger you buy, it will support the plant and the container you have in mind.

Caring for Hanging Gardens

When summer heat is intense, hanging baskets of plants must be watered at least once a day, especially if they are outdoors. The rest of the year, and in air-conditioned rooms, water once or twice a week depending on the needs of the plants. Because hanging baskets may be exposed to dry, hot air on all sides, they tend to dry out quickly. Keep the soil moist (but not soaked) for good plant growth.

The drip and overflow of water from hanging containers can be a problem. This is easy to overcome, however, by attaching saucers to the containers by wire hooks. Hanging baskets may be purchased with water-holding drip pans already attached.

Fertilizing should be delayed until the plants in the baskets are established and growing. Then,

Pots can be hung against a wall or fence. Plants here, starting at the top, are geranium (*Pelargonium hortorum*), Moses-in-the-cradle (*Rhoco spathacea*), and cineraria (*Senecio cruentis*).

Pots are held against the wall by clips which can be attached to the rim.

Hangers are available commercially, or you can make them yourself. Rope, leather, macrame, and many other types of hangers are decorative as well as practical.

29

because of the frequency of watering, some plant food is quickly washed away and must be replenished. Fertilize established plants every two to four weeks with a complete liquid fertilizer in mild solution. Apply fertilizer according to label directions, and do not exceed the manufacturer's recommendations.

Galvanized wire baskets are ideal, because of their light weight, for double baskets. Small wire hooks make it possible to suspend one basket beneath another.

Plants in hanging baskets require some grooming. Keep yellowed leaves and faded flowers removed. Baskets of annual flowers, such as morningglories and nasturtiums, can be periodically replenished with fresh seed to keep new growth and flowers continuous. Add a dozen new seeds to the basket once a month and cover them lightly with soil. Water the basket thoroughly.

Many foliage plants, such as Boston fern, Swedish ivy, or wanderingjew, may live and thrive in the same hanging basket for up to several years. All hanging baskets will eventually require fresh soil, however. When roots begin to appear on the surface of the soil or around the edges of the root ball, take the plant out of the container, trim back one-third of the top growth, and remove one-third of the soil from the root ball. Scrape residual salts (white, crusted matter) from the top of the root ball. Trim roots that protrude beyond the soil ball. Place fresh soil in the bottom of the basket and replace the plants in the basket. Fill around the root ball with fresh soil and tamp it down with a stick or trowel handle. Water the basket thoroughly.

Be sure to tend to your hanging baskets before the fall frost. Bring them in when night temperatures dip regularly into the low forties. When early spring arrives, take advantage of particularly nice days by hanging one or two of your baskets outside. Bring them in at night, however, until all danger of frost is past.

Damage from dripping water is a factor to consider with hanging baskets. A glass bowl or other type of saucer can be attached to eliminate this problem.

Terrariums

Terrariums, miniature gardens enclosed in glass containers, are more popular today than ever before. Anyone can be successful with terrarium culture; it is an essentially carefree way to grow plants. Since terrariums do well under artificial light and are not affected by low humidity, they are particularly appealing to people with little or no outdoor gardening space. Terrariums and miniature gardens also make superb gifts at any time of the year.

The variety of containers suitable for terrariums allows the indoor gardener almost infinite decorating possibilities.

Constructing the Terrarium

There are many containers that can serve as terrariums: brandy snifters, apothecary jars, aquariums, fishbowls, and bottles of all shapes and sizes. The container size is limited only by the number and scale of plants you wish to put into it. A glass container is usually preferable to plastic because glass does not scratch or discolor as easily. If a cover is not provided, you can improvise one with a piece of glass or plastic that seals tightly.

Once you have selected a container, clean it with soap and water, and dry it until it is spotless. In the bottom of the container, place a layer of clean gravel topped with a small amount of charcoal granules to aid in keeping the soil from becoming too acid. Add sterilized soil mix, available at garden supply stores, to the desired level. If the opening of the container is small, use a funnel to get the soil into the container without getting the sides dirty. To avoid splattering plants with soil, add all the soil you intend to use before you begin to set the plants. Be sure the soil is moist, but not wet, before you put it in the container. Next, set the plants in place, using long-handled spoons, forks, or sticks as necessary.

After planting, water just enough to settle the plants. Leave the terrarium uncovered for a day or two to make sure that the plants are adapting to the container; then cover the opening of the container to maintain the humidity level inside. Place the terrarium where it will receive plenty of light but no direct sunlight.

Terrariums need very little additional moisture; add only a small amount of water when plants show signs of wilting.

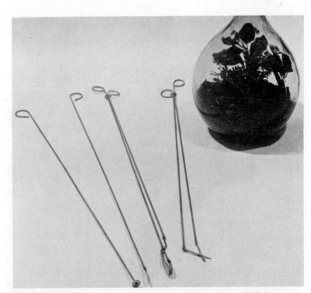

The terrarium enthusiast will need special tools for planting and maintaining miniature gardens. From left to right: soil tamper, spade, grip (for setting or removing plants), and pruning shears.

Fertilizer, if used at all, should be applied very sparingly lest the plants outgrow their container too quickly.

Either native or tropical plants may be selected for terrariums. Most small plants that grow in a damp, tree-covered forest area will do well in the moist atmosphere of a terrarium. Small house plants, such as miniature African violets, tropical ferns, ivy, and peperomia, may be combined for an easy-to-care-for terrarium. Forest mosses are also excellent terrarium candidates.

Types of Terrariums

The type of terrarium you build is determined by your selection of plants. Because a terrarium is a closed minienvironment providing a uniform climate throughout, plants requiring similar growing conditions must be chosen. In planning a terrarium, consider plants in one of two cultural groupings: those suitable for woodland terrariums and those suitable for tropical terrariums.

Woodland terrariums. The best plants for woodland terrariums can probably be found within a few miles of your home. Cover the floor of the terrarium with mosses and lichens. Not only will these create a forest floor effect, but the bits of sod will also provide anchorage for roots of other plants.

You can buy plants for a terrarium or, for a woodland terrarium, you can dig them yourself if you first obtain permission from the owner of the property where you wish to dig. Select only small, fine-textured plants for the terrarium and be sure to collect a portion of the root system with soil

To minimize cleanup, roll a sheet of paper into a cone and funnel the soil carefully into the terrarium container.

Moisten the soil before you set the plants. A squeeze bulb allows you to water the terrarium without disturbing either the soil or plants.

still attached to the roots. Place plants in a plastic sandwich bag to transport them home. Transplant them into the terrarium as soon as possible to assure their survival.

Tropical terrariums. Since most common house plants are native to the tropics, selecting plant material is not difficult; rooted cuttings or offsets of plants such as spider plant or babystears are good to begin with. Small plants with finely textured foliage are best suited to the tiny world of the terrarium.

Troubles in Miniature worlds

Wilting of terrarium plants is usually due to inadequate moisture. Water the terrarium by misting or with a squeeze bulb. Mist the plants and soil very lightly until wilting is checked and the plants look healthy again. If the terrarium tends to dry out rapidly, it may be receiving too much light and heat. Simple relocation of the terrarium will often provide the remedy.

Plants that outgrow their space in the terrarium must be removed and potted separately. Fill the empty areas with small plants which are in better proportion to the rest of the terrarium.

Prune fast-growing plants from time to time, especially if they begin to crowd other plants. This will considerably extend the life of the terrarium.

Terrariums are not permanent; eventually all the plants will outgrow the container and will need to be replaced. At this point, empty the container, clean it and start afresh with sterilized soil and new plants.

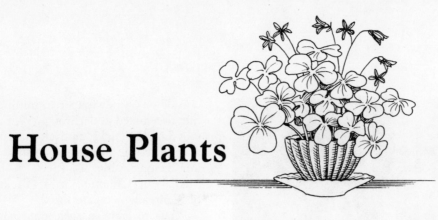

House Plants

House plants include an enormous range of plants selected for their ability to adapt to the foreign world of the indoors. House plants have enjoyed a renewed popularity in the 1970s causing the opening of a great number of greenhouses and a constantly expanding selection of plants from all over the world. Although many plants discussed in other chapters are house plants in the sense that they can be grown indoors, the discussion in this chapter is limited to those plants that are most often thought of by tradespeople and amateur growers as classic house plants.

House plants, large and small, can add dynamic character to a room.

Selecting Plants

House plants fall into two general categories: those enjoyed for their foliage characteristics, and those enjoyed for their flowers. Many plants are desirable for both foliage and flowers. Although some flowering plants, such as spathiphyllum and wax begonia, are among the easiest plants to grow, foliage plants tend to be easier to grow than most flowering plants. African violets, for instance, are definitely easy to grow, but getting them to bloom frustrates many beginning gardeners.

Never be afraid to try new plants. Commercially available house plants have been selected for marketing because of their ability to grow indoors. Plants in every category are adapted for use indoors including palms, ferns, bulbs, shrubs, annual flowers, cacti, and succulents.

The primary consideration in placing plants indoors is to satisfy the light needs of the plant. Beyond that, only a few cautions are necessary to avoid problems. Do not place plants near registers, radiators, or other heating outlets. Plants gener-

Weeping fig (*Ficus benjamina*) is one of the best indoor trees for the house plant enthusiast.

Red-margined dracaena (*Dracaena marginata*) combines the desertlike appeal of cacti and yuccas with the tropical feeling of long, sparse, wiry stems. Cascading over the sides of the container is peperomia (*P. obtusifolia*).

ally respond poorly to sudden changes in temperature and to the relentless barrage of warm dry air from heating outlets. Air conditioners, on the other hand, may benefit plants, especially if the currents of cool air are not too strong.

Avoid placing plants where they will be in the way of people passing by. Few plants respond well to being brushed against, and all plants respond very poorly to being knocked over.

Most house plants do respond well, however, to artificial lighting and a lighted planter can be the solution in a poorly lighted house. For more information on the use of artificial lighting, see "Lighting Needs" in Chapter One.

During the summer, move plants to outdoor living areas so that they may be enjoyed on porches, decks, balconies, and the like. The plants will benefit from the fresh air, dew, and rain.

Soil for House Plants

Most common house plants grow well in a loamy soil mix, consisting of equal parts garden loam, peat moss, and sand or perlite. Mix the soil outside or on newspaper to minimize the cleanup. Sift the mixed soil through ¼-inch screen to remove rocks, sticks, and clods. To kill nematodes and soil-borne disease organisms, sterilize the soil mix before using it. (See "Soils and Growing Media" in Chapter One). Packaged soil mixes have already been sterilized.

Plants to grow in sphagnum moss. Some plants grow well in sphagnum moss alone (available at garden supply stores), and therefore do not require the effort of mixing soils. Like packaged potting soils, packaged sphagnum moss is sterile. Such a peaty medium is very moisture retentive, and plants grown in it require less frequent watering than plants grown in a soil mixture. The following plants grow well in sphagnum moss:

Azalea	Gardenia, Cape jasmine
Chinese evergreen	Monstera
Dieffenbachia	Philodendron
Waxplant	

Plants to grow in water. A few plants will grow in ordinary tap water. Change the water every week to prevent plants and water from becoming rancid. Add ¼ teaspoon of mild liquid fertilizer per quart of fresh water every other time you change the water. The following plants grow well in a container with 1 to 2 inches of water:

Chinese evergreen	English ivy
Coleus	Heartleaf philodendron
Cordyline, Hawaiian ti plant	Scindapsus, Devil's ivy
	Swedish ivy
Wanderingjew	

Caring for House Plants
Watering and misting

Plants with high moisture and humidity needs should be double-potted to assure adequate irrigation.

Plants in clay containers will need to be watered more frequently than those in plastic, ceramic, or other nonporous materials.

Most house plants fall into one of two general categories based on watering needs, those plants that should be allowed to dry partially between thorough weekly waterings, and those plants that should be kept constantly moist by frequent light waterings.

The vast majority of house plants need only a thorough watering once a week. They do, however, respond well to being sprayed with a misting bottle every few days. Consult the chart at the end of this chapter to learn the moisture requirements of specific house plants.

Saucers are a must for indoor plants. Place them under pots to catch excess water and prevent staining of floors, shelves, and tables.

Fertilizing

Apply mild solutions of liquid fertilizer to most house plants every month or two from early spring to early fall, but withhold fertilizer during the late fall and winter while plants are in a dormant state.

Do not overfertilize house plants. Excess salts and fertilizer have no way to escape from the container and may burn plant roots. For instructions on making and using fertilizer solutions, see "Fertilizing" in Chapter One.

Washing and grooming

Dust and other dirt may collect on the leaves of house plants, dulling their sheen and, eventually, hampering their ability to take up carbon dioxide from the air, a function which is important for plants to survive. To keep smooth-leaved plants looking their best, wipe the leaves with a damp sponge at least once a month. This monthly sponge bath also helps prevent the buildup of insects and their larvae (immature states of the insects).

Do not attempt to sponge-bathe hairy-leaved plants or those whose leaves are fragile, such as

India false aralia (*Polyscias fruticosa*) creates an oriental effect in this jardiniere.

ferns. You may want to bring all your plants outside from time to time and spray them with the garden hose. A good hosing not only cleans the plants, it also helps control insects.

Pinch back spindly stems and dead or yellowed leaves. Pinching makes plants bushier by stimulating new growth at the points where parts have been removed. Use scissors, or pinch stems and leaf stalks between your thumb and forefinger nail.

Repotting

Remove plants from their containers occasionally to see if roots have become matted and entangled around their soil balls, a condition called "pot-bound." A few plants, including spathiphyllum, geraniums, African violets, gloxinia, and several palm species, seem to perform best when they are slightly pot-bound, but these plants are the exception. Most plants grow poorly when they are pot-bound.

Repot overcrowded plants in the spring or whenever they need such attention. (See "Potting and Repotting" in Chapter One.)

Most house plants grow best under well-lighted conditions. This large window greenhouse provides an ideal environment for plants.

Saddleleaf philodendron (*Philodendron selluom*) is a dramatic house plant, displayed alone or with other plants.

African violets (*Saintpaulia sp.*) need steady light in order to flower well.

Insect and Disease Control

Inspect plants regularly for insect or disease problems, and segregate afflicted plants immediately to prevent the spread of these problems to healthy plants. Many house plants need only to be sponged down or washed in soapy water to remove insects. (See Chapter Fifteen, Problems in Container Gardens.) Persistent insects and diseases may require the use of a chemical pesticide. Sprays of malathion and Sevin will eliminate the majority of insect pests. General purpose fungicides include maneb, zineb, and Captan.

Deal with plant disorders as soon as you detect them; most cannot wait.

Propagating House Plants

You can start new plants from old ones by several easy methods. Portions of a stem with a few leaves will form roots in a mixture of perlite and peat moss. This method, called "stem cuttings," will work on most common house plants. Begonias and several other popular plants can be grown from portions of a leaf, termed "leaf cuttings," placed in a perlite and peat moss rooting mixture. You can propagate some plants by rooting 1-inch sections of the main stem. Other easy methods of starting new plants include air-layering, root divisions, and offsets. The chart at the end of this chapter suggests the easiest methods of propagating specific plants.

Many house plants can be rooted from stem cuttings. Make cuttings just above a leaf or leaf node. Each cutting should be no longer than 4 or 5 inches.

Insert the cutting in a rooting mixture of equal parts peat moss and sand (or perlite).

Plantlets growing at the ends of elongated stems of spider plant are called offsets. To propagate these, snip them from the mother plant and pot them individually.

Some plants, such as gloxinia, can be rooted simply by placing the cuttings in water. Cover the top of the container with aluminum foil to hold the cutting in the container. Other plants that root in water include African violet, wax begonia, fuchsia, English ivy, Swedish ivy, philodendron, and most wanderingjews.

One of the simplest methods of propagating plants is to divide the roots at repotting time and pot each division individually. If you cannot pull the roots apart, use a sharp knife to cut them.

Air-layering

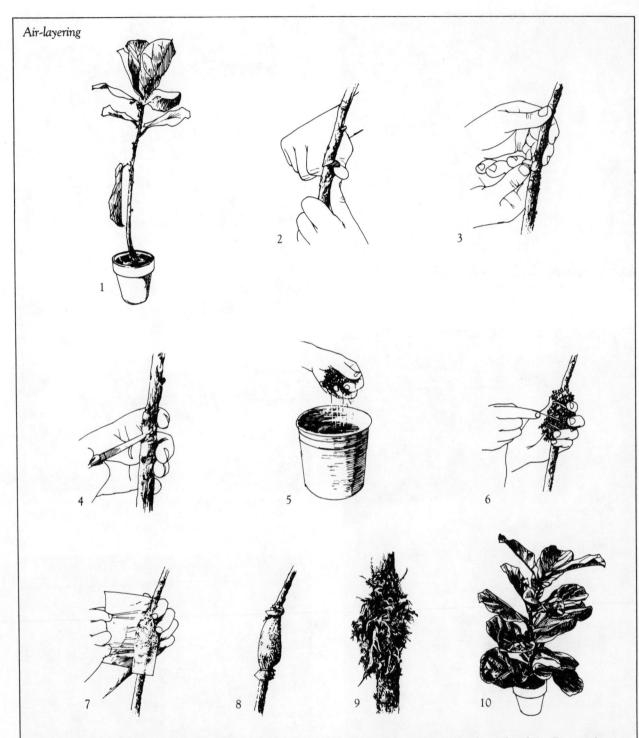

When the lower stem of a large plant becomes bare and unsightly, it may be necessary to air-layer the plant. First, make a slanting cut about halfway into the stem several inches below the healthy section of the plant. Hold the wound open by inserting a piece of a toothpick. If you use a root-inducing hormone, apply it at this stage. Use a knife or other flat object to apply the hormone powder to surfaces of the wound. Take a handful of moist sphagnum moss. Wrap the moss around the wound. Leave the toothpick in place to keep wound surfaces exposed. Secure the moss with string. Wrap cellophane around the moss and secure it above and below the wound. After a few weeks, roots will form inside the moss ball. Remove the cellophane, cut the stem just below the new root ball, and pot the new plant.

House Plant Culture Guide

Latin Name	Common Name	Light	Soil	Water	Propagation
Acalypha hispida, A. wilkesiana macafaeana	Chenille plant, Copperleaf	Direct sun or bright indirect; 800–1000fc	Loamy	Moist at all times	Stem cuttings of new growth in summer
Aeschynanthus parvifolius	Lipstick plant, Basket vine	Direct sun or bright indirect; 800–1000fc	Peaty loam	Moist at all times	Stem cuttings in spring or early summer
Aglaonema simplex	Chinese evergreen	Medium or low; 150–300fc	Peaty loam or plain water	Moist at all times	Stem cuttings or root divisions at any time of year
Aphelandra squarrosa louisae	Aphelandra	Bright indirect; 600–800fc	Peaty loam	Constantly moist spring to fall; partially dry between thorough waterings in winter; use pebble tray to raise humidity	Stem cuttings in spring or early summer
Aspidistra eliator	Aspidistra, Cast-iron plant	Medium or low; 150–300fc	Loamy	Slightly moist at all times	Root division in spring
Begonia coccinea, B. rex, B. semperflorens	Angelwing begonia, Rex begonia, Wax begonia	Bright indirect during growing season; 600–800fc; Direct sun in winter; 800–1000fc	Peaty loam	Slightly moist from spring to fall; partially dry between thorough waterings in winter; use pebble tray to raise humidity for B. rex	B. rex: leaf or stem cuttings at any time of year; B. semperflorens; stem cuttings in summer or fall, seeds at any time of year
Beloperone guttata	Shrimp plant	Direct sun; 800–1000fc	Loamy	Partially dry between thorough waterings	Cuttings from tips of stems at any time of year
Brassaia actinophylla	Schefflera, Australian umbrella tree, Octopus tree	Direct sun or bright indirect; 800–1000fc	Loamy	Partially dry between thorough waterings	Seeds
Calathea makoyana	Peacock plant	Medium; 400–600fc	Sandy peat plus loam; crushed charcoal in bottom of container	Moist at all times; use pebble tray to raise humidity	Stem cuttings, tubers, or root divisions; all best in spring
Chlorophytum comosum	Airplane plant, Spider plant	Bright indirect or medium; 600–800fc	Loamy	Slightly moist at all times	Plantlets at end of elongated shoots at any time of year
Cissus rhombifolius	Grape ivy	Bright indirect or medium; 600–800fc	Loamy	Slightly moist at all times	Stem cuttings at any time of year
Codiaeum variegattum pictum	Croton	Direct sun; 1000–1200fc	Loamy	Slightly moist at all times	Stem cuttings or air-layering in spring
Coleus blumei	Common coleus	Direct sun or bright indirect; 800–1000fc	Loamy	Moist at all times	Stem cuttings or seeds at any time of year
Cordyline terminalis	Hawaiian ti plant	Direct sun; 1000–1200fc	Loamy	Moist at all times; use pebble tray to raise humidity	Air-layering, root 3-inch sections of main stem at any time of year

House Plant Culture Guide (continued)

Latin Name	Common Name	Light	Soil	Water	Propagation
Dieffenbachia sp.	Dieffenbachia, Dumb cane	Medium or low; 150–300fc	Loamy	Partially dry between thorough waterings; do not overwater	Stem cuttings or air-layering any time of year
Dizygotheca elegantissima	False aralia	Bright indirect or medium; 400–600fc	Loamy	Slightly moist at all times	Stem cuttings in spring or early summer
Dracaena fragrans D. marginata D. sanderiana	Corn plant Red-margined dracaena Sander's dracaena	Medium; 400–600fc	Sandy loam	Moist at all times	Stem cuttings or air-layering at any time of year
Euphorbia pulcherrima	Poinsettia	Dark place after bloom, full sun April to October; total dark 12 hrs./night October to December	Loamy	Reduce after bloom until April; moist at all times April to January	Stem cuttings of new growth in summer
Fatsia japonica	Japanese aralia	Direct sun or bright indirect; 800–1000fc	Loamy	Slightly moist at all times	Root suckers at base of plants in spring
Ficus benjamina F. elastica F. pandurata	Weeping fig India-rubber tree Fiddleleaf fig	Medium; 400–600fc	Loamy	Slightly moist at all times	Stem cuttings or air-layering at any time of year
Fittonia sp.	Fittonia, Mosaic plant	Medium or low; 400–600fc	Loamy	Moist at all times; use pebble tray to raise humidity	Stem cuttings in spring or summer
Fuchsia sp.	Fuchsia	Bright indirect in summer, direct sun rest of year; 600–800fc	Peaty loam	Moist at all times	Stem cuttings of new growth in summer or early fall
Gynura sarmentosa	Gynura, Purple passion vine	Direct sun or bright indirect; 800–1000fc	Loamy	Slightly moist at all times	Cuttings from ends of branches at any time of year
Hedera helix	English ivy	Bright indirect, medium, or low; 400–600fc	Loamy	Slightly moist at all times	Stem cuttings at any time of year
Helxine soleirolii	Babystears	Medium; 400–600fc	Loamy	Moist at all times; use pebble tray to raise humidity	Stem cuttings or root divisions at any time of year
Hoya carnosa	Hoya, Waxplant	Bright indirect or medium; 600–800fc	Loamy	Constantly moist in summer and fall; partially dry between thorough waterings in late winter and spring	Stem cuttings or air-layering at any time of year
Maranta leuconeura	Maranta, Prayer plant	Medium or low; 300–600fc	Loamy	Medium moist at all times	Root divisions in spring when repotting
Monstera deliciosa	Splitleaf philodendron, Swiss cheese plant, Hurricane plant, Monstera	Bright indirect or medium; 400–600fc	Peaty loam	Slightly moist at all times	Stem cuttings or air-layering at any time of year; also from seed of fruit borne on plants grown in tropics

House Plant Culture Guide (continued)

Latin Name	Common Name	Light	Soil	Water	Propagation
Nephthytis triphylla (formerly Synogonium triphylla)	African evergreen, Arrowhead vine, Synogonium	Medium or low; 300–400fc	Loamy	Slightly moist at all times	Stem cuttings at any time of year
Pandanus veitchii	Screwpine, Pandanus	Bright indirect or medium; 400–600fc	Loamy	Fairly dry between thorough waterings	Root divisions
Peperomia sp.	Peperomy, Silver dollar plant, Pepperface, Watermelon begonia	Bright indirect or medium; 400–600fc	Peaty loam	Partially dry between thorough waterings	Stem or leaf cuttings at any time of year; root divisions in spring when repotting
Philodendron cordata P. hastatum P. selluom	Heartleaf philodendron Spadeleaf philodendron Saddleleaf philodendron	Bright indirect or medium; 400–600fc	Peaty loam; P. cordata also in plain water	Slightly moist at all times	Stem cuttings (in solid medium or water) or air-layering at any time of year
Pilea cadieri P. microphylla P. involucrata	Aluminum plant Artillery plant Panamiga	Bright indirect or medium; 400–600fc	Peaty loam	Slightly moist at all times	Stem cuttings at any time of year; root divisions in spring when repotting
Plectranthus sp.	Swedish ivy, Variegated spurflower	Bright indirect; 600–800fc	Loamy	Slightly moist at all times	Stem cuttings (in solid medium or water) at any time of year; root divisions in spring when repotting; stem cuttings may not reproduce variegated foliage
Polyscias balfouriana	Balfour aralia	Direct sun or bright indirect; 800–1000fc	Loamy	Slightly moist at all times	Stem cuttings at any time of year
Rhoeo spathacea	Moses-in-the-cradle	Medium; 400–600fc	Loamy	Slightly moist at all times	Root divisions, suckers, or seeds at any time of year
Saintpaulia sp.	African violet	Bright indirect (avoid direct sun); 800–1000fc	Loamy	Slightly moist at all times; use pebble tray to raise humidity	Leaf cuttings, leaf plus petiole (stem of leaf), root divisions, or seeds at any time of year
Saxifraga sarmentosa	Strawberry geranium, Strawberry begonia, Mother-of-thousands	Bright indirect or medium; 400–600fc	Loamy	Partially dry between thorough waterings	Plantlets at ends of elongated stems at any time of year
Scindapsus aureus	Devil's ivy	Medium; 400–600fc	Loamy soil or plain water	Partially dry between thorough waterings	Stem cuttings at any time of year
Sinningia speciosa	Gloxinia	Bright indirect (avoid direct sun); 800–1000fc	Peaty loam	Slightly moist at all times	Leaf cuttings, seeds, or tubers at any time of year
Solanum pseudocapsicum	Jerusalem cherry	Direct sun or bright indirect; 800–1000fc	Loamy	Partially dry between thorough waterings	Annual must be grown from seed; discard plants after fruiting
Spathiphyllum clevelandii	Spathiphyllum	Medium to low; 400–600fc bright indirect in winter; 600–800fc	Peaty loam	Moist at all times	Root divisions at any time of year
Tolmeia mensyi	Piggyback plant, Pick-a-back	Bright indirect or medium; 600–800fc	Loamy	Moist at all times; use pebble tray to raise humidity	Leaf plus petiole (leaf stem) of leaf bearing plantlet; mother leaf inserted so that leaf rests on surface of rooting medium
Tradescantia fluminensis Tripogandra multiflora Zebrina pendula	Wanderingjew	Bright indirect or medium; 600–800fc	Loamy	Medium moist at all times	Stem cuttings (in solid medium or water) at any time of year

Cacti and Succulents

Cacti and succulents are among the best plants for container gardens. Because of their ability to grow under hot, dry desert conditions, cacti and succulents make ideal house plants. Granted, the average home is not desertlike, but the amount of moisture in the air is quite low. For this reason, many tropical or forest plants do not adapt well to conditions inside the home, whereas cacti and other succulents may find indoor conditions quite satisfactory.

Any plant with thick, fleshy leaves or stems that is capable of storing large quantities of water in those fleshy parts is called a *succulent*. Although succulents do not constitute a family in themselves, over 8,000 species of plants are classified as succulents. Some well-known succulents include jade plant, echeveria, sedum, and crown-of-thorns. Also included in the succulent group are over 2,000 species of cacti.

Cacti generally are leafless plants with thick, fleshy stems lined with prickly spines. The stems store large quantities of moisture which enables the plant to survive through weeks of rainless desert weather. Most cacti have shallow roots which permit immediate absorption of the scant amount of rain they are accustomed to receiving. Although to many the intriguing forms in which cacti grow are bizarre, the fascination of these dramatic plants increases as they become more familiar.

The range of plant sizes and forms among succulents is vast. Succulents can be used in nearly every type of display situation from miniature gardens and hanging baskets to large upright cacti for a striking effect in a corner of a room.

Cacti, whether alone or in numbers, are among the world's most captivating and unusual plants.

Cacti and succulents make superb container plants for indoors or out. Shown here are (clockwise from upper left) miniature goldenstar cactus (*Mammillaria elongata minima*), euphorbia (*Euphorbia* sp.), and burrostail (*Sedum morganianum*).

Caring for Cacti and Succulents

Cacti and succulents are among the easiest house plants to care for. They require less watering than most plants, and usually require less frequent repotting due to their slow rate of growth.

Give a cactus the sunniest location in your home. Other succulents also need a bright location, but do not expose them to direct sunlight; the leaves are easily scorched. A major difference between cacti and other succulents is that most succulents have not lost their leaves in the course of evolution, whereas cacti have. Plants with leaves are generally more susceptible to scorching than those without leaves.

If you use artificial light, provide at least 800 foot-candles for cacti, 500 to 800 foot-candles for other succulents.

Soil for cacti and succulents should be a sandy mix. Mix 2 parts sand or perlite with 1 part loam and 1 part peat moss. As for other house plants, soil for succulents and cacti should be sterilized (see "Soils and Growing Media" in Chapter One). A little charcoal in the soil increases the moisture-absorption capacity of the soil mixture, further reducing the danger of overwatering.

The results of overwatering succulents are often fatal. Cacti have developed in areas where rainfall is consistently sparse and, as a consequence, do not have the type of feeder roots that can take up a great quantity of moisture at one time. Other succulents, by contrast, have developed in climates that are subject to heavy rainfall followed

Use newspaper, paper towels, or gloves when potting or repotting cacti to avoid pricking yourself on the sharp spines.

by extended periods of drought. Too much water causes cacti and succulents to become mushy and to eventually die.

Depending on the size of the plant and the type container used, most succulents need watering every 3 to 5 days during the growing season (February to November) if the pot is of clay or other porous material. Those in plastic or ceramic containers require even less watering. Allow soil to dry partially between waterings but not so dry that the plants shrivel.

During the dormant season (November to February), water cacti every 10 to 14 days or just enough to keep them from shriveling. Water only on dry, sunny days when the plant's roots and moisture-absorbing tissues are most receptive. Use lukewarm water or water that has been allowed to sit for an hour or two at room temperature, cold water can cause minor injury to some succulents.

Average home temperatures are suitable for succulents. If, however, you expect your cactus to bloom, provide cool temperatures during the winter, about 45° at night and 50° to 65° during the day. A sunny, enclosed porch where the temperature does not drop below 45° is an ideal place to winter your cactus. A sunny basement window may also be a good location.

Fertilize cacti and succulents once each year in the early spring with slow-release fertilizer. Cottonseed meal is a good slow-release, organic fertilizer. Other suitable fertilizers are commercially available. Slow-release fertilizers provide smaller quantities of nourishment to the plant over a long period of time.

Repot succulents, including cacti, at least once every 2 years. The best time to repot them is in

A strawberry jar makes a good container for succulents. Sedum, shown here, grows in the top and in the side pockets, too.

the spring as new growth begins, but if your plants become too crowded, do not wait until spring to repot them. To avoid pricking yourself on cactus spines, use gloves or a folded sheet of newspaper to hold the stalk. Turn the plant and container upside down and remove the plant from its container. Select a new container at least 2 inches larger in diameter than the old one. If the plant is globular, the pot should be 1 inch greater in diameter than the plant. Good drainage is crucial for cacti and succulents, so be sure to provide a 1-inch layer of pebbles or charcoal in the bottom of the new container. Charcoal absorbs excess moisture which could be harmful if left to stand around the roots.

Repot succulents other than cacti in the same way you would other house plants. (See "Potting and Repotting" in Chapter One.)

How to Make a Dish Garden

A dish garden creates a miniature world of cacti and succulents. Use a bowl or other shallow container and loamy soil mix. Cover the mix with about 1 inch of fine sand to create a desert effect.

Group plants of similar size together and use taller plants as accents within the dish garden.

Do not handle cacti with your bare hands; wear gloves or use forceps.

You may want to embellish the dish garden with two or three stones to enhance the desert effect.

Propagating Cacti and Succulents

Propagate cacti and succulents from divisions, stem and leaf cuttings, and seeds. Many of these plants produce offsets (young plants) around the base of the mother plant and these need only be removed from the mother plant and potted. If the plantlets do not separate easily in your hands, use a sharp knife to make the divisions.

Leaf cuttings may be rooted in sand or perlite mixed with an equal amount of soil. Make cuttings of a whole leaf or part of a leaf. Allow the cut end to dry out for 2 or 3 days before inserting it in the rooting medium. Crassula, gasteria, haworthia, sansevieria, and kalanchoe are all easy to propagate by this method. The best time to take cuttings is in spring just as new growth is beginning.

Grafting is another popular technique for propagating cacti. Globular cacti or clusters of small, rounded cacti can be grafted onto flat, upright stems of opuntia, euphorbia, or cereus cactus. Grafting is the only sure way of rooting difficult species. This type of culture often promotes vigorous, dynamic growth.

Propagate echeveria (*Echeveria*) and many other succulents simply by snipping off plantlets growing along the stem of the mother plant.

Pot the plantlets in their own containers.

Most succulents, including echeveria (*Echeveria*), can also be propagated from leaf cuttings. Either a whole leaf or a section of a leaf can form roots when placed in a rooting medium of equal parts sand (or perlite) and peat moss. Poke a hole in the medium to insert each leaf section.

Grafting Cactus

A grafted cactus is composed of a root and stem (understock) and top (scion). Cathedral cactus (left) is one of the commonly used understocks. Nearly any appropriately sized scion can be grafted successfully to a sturdy understock.

After removing the roots from the scion, make another thin slice with a sharp knife at the bottom of the scion.

Make a thin slice on the top of the understock where the scion will come in contact.

Using a paper towel to handle the prickly scion, press the freshly cut surface of the scion against the fresh cut in the understock. For the graft to be successful, the diameter of the slice in the scion should match the diameter of the slice at the bottom of the scion.

Secure the scion on the understock with rubber bands until the graft union has formed.

Cactus Culture Guide

Latin Name	Common Name	Size and Form	Adaptation	Light	Soil	Water
Aporocactus flagelliformis	Rattail cactus	Medium; pendulous stems	Indoors, hanging basket; Outdoors, zone 10	Direct sun or bright indirect; 800–1000fc	Sandy loam plus crushed charcoal	Nearly dry between thorough waterings; reduce water in winter
Cephalocereus senilis	Old man cactus	Small to medium; hairy, columnar	Indoors, dish garden, windowsill; Outdoors, zones 9–10	Direct sun or bright indirect; 800–1000fc	Sandy loam plus crushed charcoal	Nearly dry between thorough waterings; reduce water in winter
Echinopsis multiplex (formerly Cereus multiplex)	Pink Easterlily cactus	Small to medium; ribbed, globular	Indoors, windowsill	Direct sun or bright indirect; 800–1000fc	Sandy loam plus crushed charcoal	Nearly dry between thorough waterings; reduce water in winter
Gymnocalycium mihanovichii	Plaid cactus	Small; ribbed, globular	Indoors, dish garden, desert terrariums	Direct sun or bright indirect; 800–1000fc	Sandy loam plus crushed charcoal	Nearly dry between thorough waterings; reduce water in winter
Lobivia aurea	Golden Easterlily cactus, Cob cactus	Small; blunt, cylindrical	Indoors, dish garden, windowsill; Outdoors, zones 9–10	Direct sun or bright indirect; 800–1000fc	Sandy loam plus crushed charcoal	Nearly dry between thorough waterings; reduce water in winter
Mammillaria camptotricha M. elongata M. hahniana	Birdsnest cactus Goldenstar cactus Old lady cactus	Small; fingerlike stems	Indoors, dish garden, windowsill; Outdoors, zones 9–10	Direct sun or bright indirect; 800–1000fc	Sandy loam plus crushed charcoal	Nearly dry between thorough waterings; reduce water in winter
Notocactus leninghausii N. scopa	Goldenball cactus Silverball cactus	Small; blunt, cylindrical	Indoors, dish gardens, windowsill	Direct sun or bright indirect; 800–1000fc	Sandy loam plus crushed charcoal	Nearly dry between thorough waterings; reduce water in winter
Opuntia basilaris O. microdasys	Beavertail cactus Bunny ears	Large; flat oval stems	Indoors, tub or large pot; Outdoors, O. basilaris, zones 5–10; O. macrodasys, zones 8–10	Direct sun or bright indirect; 800–1000fc	Sandy loam plus crushed charcoal	Nearly dry between thorough waterings; reduce water in winter
Yucca aloifolia	Yucca, Spanish bayonet	Medium to large	Indoors, large pot or tub; Outdoors, raised planter, zones 8–10	Medium to bright indirect; 400–800fc	Loamy	Partially dry between thorough waterings; reduce water in winter
Zygocactus truncatus	Christmas cactus	Medium to flat; cascading stems	Indoors, hanging basket, mantel; Outdoors, zone 10	Bright indirect or medium; 600–800fc	Sandy loam plus leaf mold	Slightly moist at all times; dry between thorough waterings in winter

Succulent Culture Guide

Latin Name	Common Name	Form	Color	Adaptation	Light	Water	Temperature in °F.
Adromischus maculatus	Calico hearts	Cluster of small, thick, cordate leaves	Gray green spotted brown	Indoors, windowsill Outdoors, zones 9–10	Direct sun or bright indirect; 800–1000fc	Partially dry between thorough waterings; reduce water in winter	50°–70°
Aeonium arboreum	Aeonium	Large rosettes, up to 2' wide	Pale green	Indoors, tub, stationary planter; Outdoors, zones 9–10 west	Direct sun or bright indirect; 1000–1200fc	Partially dry between thorough waterings; reduce water in winter	50°–70°
Agave americana	Century plant, American aloe	Cluster of thick, swordlike leaves	Shades of green	Indoors, tub, raised planter; Outdoors, zones 6–10	Direct sun or bright indirect; 1000–1200fc	Partially dry between thorough waterings; reduced water in winter	50°–70°
Aloe sp.	Variegated aloe, True aloe, Burn plant	Fan of thick, elongated leaves	Gray green or variegated	Indoors, shallow containers; Outdoors, zones 9–10	Direct sun or bright indirect; 1000–1200fc	Partially dry between thorough waterings; reduce water in winter	50°–70°
Crassula argentea *C. arborescens*	Jade plant Silver dollar	Small tree, Small, fleshy, rounded leaves	Gray green leaves; brown trunk	Indoors, medium to large pot; Outdoors, tub, *C. argentea,* zone 10; *C. arborescens,* zones 9–10	Direct sun or bright indirect; 1000–1200fc	Partially dry between thorough waterings; reduce water in winter	50°–80°
Echeveria elegans *E. pulvinata*	Mexican snowball Plush plant	Rosette of thick oval leaves	Pale green	Indoors, windowsill, dish garden; Outdoors, zones 9–10	Direct sun or bright indirect; 600–1000fc	Partially dry between thorough waterings; reduce water in winter	50°–70°
Euphorbia lactea *E. splendens*	Milkstriped euphorbia Crown-of-thorns.	Large, spiny, triangular stems, candelabra form; *E. splendens,* shrublike, thorny, spreading arms	Dark green stems streaked white; *E. splendens,* light green	Indoors, large pot or tub, *E. splendens,* hanging or cascading; Outdoors, zone 10	Direct sun or bright indirect; 600–1000fc	Partially dry between thorough waterings; reduce water in winter	50°–80°

Succulent Culture Guide (continued)

Latin Name	Common Name	Form	Color	Adaptation	Light	Water	Temperature in °F.
Gasteria verrucosa	Oxtongue gasteria	Rosette of thick, elongated leaves	Dark green spotted white	Indoors, medium shallow pot, dish garden; Outdoors, zone 10 west	Direct sun or bright indirect; 600–1000fc	Partially dry between thorough waterings; reduce water in winter	50°–70°
Haworthia fasciata	Zebra	Rosette of long, fleshy, pointed leaves	Dark green; horizontal white stripes	Indoors, dish garden, desert terrarium; Outdoors, zone 10	Bright indirect or medium; 400–600fc	Partially dry between thorough waterings; reduce water in winter	50°–70°
Kalanchoe blossfeldiana	Kalanchoe, Panda plant	Leaf rosettes at ends of weak, leaning stems	Pale green	Indoors, medium pot; Outdoors, zone 10	Direct sun or bright indirect; 1000–1200fc	Partially dry between thorough waterings	50°–70°
Pachyphytum oviferum	Moonstones, Sugared almonds	Small rosette of tightly clustered oval leaves	Pale green	Indoors, dish garden, desert terrarium; Outdoors, zone 10	Direct sun or bright indirect; 1000–1200fc	Partially dry between thorough waterings; reduce water in winter	50°–70°
Sansevieria trifasciata	Snake plant, Mother-in-law tongue	Fleshy, upright, straplike leaves	Dark green; white variegation	Indoors, medium pot; Outdoors, zone 10	Medium to low; 150–300fc	Partially dry between thorough waterings; reduce water in winter	60°–85°
Sedum morganianum	Burrostail	Trailing stems thickly lined with small oval leaves	Pale green	Indoors, hanging basket; Outdoors, zone 10	Direct sun or bright indirect; 1000–1200fc	Partially dry between thorough waterings; reduce water in winter	50°–70°
Sempervivum tectorum	Hen-and-chickens	Leaf rosettes resembling echeveria; numerous offsets at base	Pale green	Indoors, dish garden, windowsill; Outdoors, zones 4–10	Direct sun or bright indirect; 1000–1200fc	Partially dry between thorough waterings; reduce water in winter	50°–70°

Ferns

Anyone who keeps potted plants probably owns at least one fern. Although ferns are not difficult to grow, they do demand precise soil, watering, and other care. Their somewhat exacting culture is simplified by remembering their natural habitat: moist, shady woods. As house plants, ferns are incomparable for their ability to bring the feeling of the forest indoors; no plant imports a mass of greenery into the home more effectively than a large fern. From the delicate, airy fronds of the maidenhair fern (*Adiantum* sp), to a massive staghorn fern (*Platycerium bifurcatum*), ferns can be used decoratively in pots or hanging baskets. Ferns are also used in bouquets and arrangements of cut flowers. To gain familiarity with the needs of ferns, beginning gardeners should start with varieties of the sword or Boston fern.

Many species of fern are available from garden supply stores and greenhouses. Some ferns are easy to transplant from the woods for use in permanent outdoor containers. Few native species, however, make satisfactory house plants.

Maidenhair ferns (*Adiantum* sp.) are handsome small plants.

Caring for Ferns

It is important to provide the correct soil and growing conditions for container-grown ferns. Soil must be rich in organic matter and kept evenly moist. Cool temperatures, medium to high humidity, and filtered shade are all necessary for success with ferns. Once the correct conditions are provided, ferns are among the least demanding of all indoor plants.

Locate ferns in windows with a northern exposure, or in bathrooms, hallways, or rooms which receive bright, indirect light but no direct sunlight. Bathrooms and kitchens are recommended because the atmosphere is usually more humid than in other rooms.

Boston ferns (*Nephrolepis exaltata bostoniensis*) are best displayed in hanging baskets.

Staghorn ferns (*Platycerium bifurcatum*) are quite effective hanging from trees where their lush foliage looks most natural.

"Fluffy Duffy" is a popular variety of Boston fern.

Mix garden loam with leaf mold, compost, peat moss, or ground fir bark to obtain the peaty soil required for ferns. Like all soil for container-grown plants, soil for ferns should be sterilized. (See "Soils and Growing Media" in Chapter One.)

Provide a container with drainage outlets. If drainage is adequate, it is nearly impossible to overwater ferns. Keep the soil moist (but not soaked), and ferns will thrive.

Fertilizer requirements for ferns potted in com-

Asparagus fern (*Asparagus sprengerii*) is not a true fern but is often displayed with ferns. Its airy foliage softens the rigid lines of planters, fences, and pavement in this yard.

post are minimal. Apply fertilizer once each month during the growing season, but withhold fertilizer from November to February. Fish emulsion is a good fertilizer for ferns, but any other commonly available house plant food is also satisfactory.

Propagating Ferns

Repot ferns annually in the spring and divide crowns to obtain several plants. If the crown (top of the root system from which stems grow) does not easily pull apart by hand, cut it into sections with a sharp knife. Pot each section of the crown individually.

Propagation of most ferns is done by dividing crowns at repotting time. Replant the new clumps at the same depth at which they were previously growing. Ferns are also propagated from spores which appear as brownish rust on undersides of the fronds. Growing ferns from spores is an exacting process and not altogether practical unless you have a greenhouse and a fair amount of patience.

Insects and diseases are rarely a problem on mature ferns. Be on the lookout, however, for scale insects. If the infestation is light, pick the insects off by hand or spray them off with a sink or garden hose. Serious infestation may require the use of a chemical insecticide, such as diazinon or dimethoate (Cygon).

51

Fern Culture Guide

Latin Name	Common Name	Size	Adaptation	Light	Soil	Water	Temperature in °F.
Adiantum sp.	Maidenhair fern	Small to medium	Indoors; Outdoors, zones 9–10	Low; 150–300fc	Loamy plus leaf mold	Moist at all times; partially dry during winter	50°–70°
Aglaomorpha meyenianum	Bearspaw fern	Medium to large	Indoors; Outdoors, zone 10	Bright indirect or medium; 400–600fc	Loamy or peaty plus leaf mold	Moist at all times	50°–80°
Asparagus meyerii, A. plumosus, A. sprengerii	Asparagus fern, Foxtail asparagus fern, Sprenger asparagus fern	Small to medium	Indoors; Outdoors, zones 8–10	Bright indirect or medium; 400–600fc	Loamy	Slightly moist at all times	50°–75°
Asplenium bulbiferum, A. nidis	Mother fern, Birdsnest fern	Medium	Indoors; Outdoors, zone 10	Low to medium 150–300fc	Loamy plus leaf mold	Moist at all times; partially dry during winter	50°–70°
Cibotium schiedei	Mexican tree fern	Large	Indoors; Outdoors, zone 10	Bright indirect or medium; 400–600fc	Loamy plus leaf mold	Slightly moist at all times	50°–70°
Cyathea arborea	Tree fern	Small to medium	Indoors; Outdoors, zone 10	Bright indirect; 600–800fc	Peaty	Very moist at all times	50°–70°
Cyrtomium falcatum (formerly Aspidium falcatum)	Japanese holly fern	Small to medium	Indoors; Outdoors, zone 10	Low to medium; 150–300fc	Loamy	Slightly moist at all times	40°–70°
Davallia fejeensis, D. trichomanioides	Rabbitsfoot fern, Squirrelsfoot fern	Small to medium	Indoors, hanging basket (pin fronds to soil to create cascade)	Low to medium; 150–300fc	Loamy or peaty plus fir bark	Slightly moist at all times	50°–80°
Humata tyermannii	Bearsfoot fern	Small to medium	Indoors, hanging basket; Outdoors, zone 10	Bright indirect or medium; 300–500fc	Loamy plus fir bark or leaf mold	Slightly moist at all times	50°–70°
Lygodium japonicum	Japanese climbing fern	Large	Indoors, hanging basket; Outdoors, zones 8–10	Bright indirect or medium; 400–600fc	Peaty, acid plus leaf mold, fir bark	Moist at all times	50°–70°
Nephrolepis exaltata, N. exaltata bostoniensis, N. exaltata whitmanii	Sword fern, Boston fern, Fluffy-ruffle fern	Medium to large	Indoors, hanging basket; Outdoors, zone 10	Bright indirect or medium; 400–600fc	Loamy plus fir bark or leaf mold	Slightly moist at all times	50°–70°
Pellaea rotundifolia	New Zealand cliffbrake fern	Medium	Indoors; Outdoors, zone 10	Bright indirect or medium; 400–600fc	Loamy plus leaf mold	Slightly moist at all times	50°–70°
Platycerium bifurcatum	Staghorn fern	Medium to large	Indoors, mounted on wall	Bright indirect or medium; 400–600fc	Sphagnum moss	Moist at all times	50°–70°

Fern Culture Guide *(continued)*

Latin Name	Common Name	Size	Adaptation	Light	Soil	Water	Temperature in °F.
Polypodium aureum	Golden polypody fern, Haresfoot fern	Medium to large	Indoors, hanging basket; Outdoors, zone 10	Bright indirect or medium; 400–600fc	Loamy or peaty plus fir bark or leaf mold	Slightly moist at all times	50°–70°
Polystichum acrostichoides	Christmas fern	Medium	Indoors, hanging basket; Outdoors, zones 4–9	Bright indirect, or medium; 400–600fc	Loamy, acid, peaty; rich in leaf mold or humus	Moist at all times during growing season; partially dry between thorough waterings in winter	45°–70°
Pteris cretica *P. ensiformis victoriae*	Table fern, Stove fern, Cretan brake fern Victoria fern	Small to medium	Indoors; Outdoors, zone 10	Low to medium; 150–300fc	Loamy plus leaf mold	Slightly moist at all times	30°–70°
Woodwardia orientalis	Oriental chain fern	Large	Indoors; Outdoors, zone 10	Bright indirect or medium; 400–600fc	Loamy plus leaf mold or fir bark	Moist at all times	50°–70°

Palms and Palmlike Plants

Palms, especially large ones, can inject your living room with tropical elegance faster than any other group of plants. Palms create an exotic atmosphere and can play a strong role in the overall character of a room.

In the southern portions of the United States, palms can be enjoyed in outdoor planters year-round, but gardeners in the rest of the country will be interested in palms for indoors. For maximum effect, feature large palms alone, placing them in corners and in front of large areas of bare wall.

Selecting Palms

Some of the least demanding palms are also among the most interesting. Popular palms, such as the parlor palm, or paradise palm, make superb house and office plants. Purchase young plants and watch them grow to ceiling height in 20 years, or start with more mature specimens and achieve dramatic effects instantly.

The following plants are recommended for beginners:

Lady palm	Sentry palm
Parlor palm	Paradise palm
Neanthe palm	Date palm

While young, parlor palms make delightful accent plants for small places, such as end tables or window sills.

Caring for Palms

Palms, like ferns, are not difficult to grow provided their few rigid requirements are met. Some palms, such as the parlor palm *Chamaedorea elegans*, make ideal house plants because of their slow rate of growth and ability to tolerate low light conditions. Light needs may vary significantly among the palm group, however, from low light to at least 4 or 5 hours of direct sunlight daily. Many respond well to artificial lighting.

Most palms prefer moist to very moist soil. Soil for some palmlike plants, however, should be allowed to become partially dry between thorough waterings. Such a plant is the elephant-foot tree, or ponytail palm (*Beaucarnea recurvata*), which is

Palms add a special touch to a room. Featured here is a parlor palm. (*Chamaedorea elegans*).

Sago palm (*Cycas revoluta*) is not a true palm but creates the effect of a palm. Locate sago palms in bright indirect light but not in direct sunlight.

not a true palm. The tree palms require light watering every two or three days to keep the soil moist, but make sure the container has adequate drainage so that roots will not stand in soggy soil.

Moisture-loving tropical plants such as palms respond well to misting at least once or twice a week. Humidity can be further improved by placing potted plants on a pebble tray. (See "Temperature and Humidity" in Chapter One).

To keep plants a manageable size, fertilize them sparingly. Mix slow-release fertilizer into the soil when you pot or repot plants, but do not begin routinely feeding new plants for 8 months to 1 year. Thereafter, fertilize plants with liquid fertilizer solution three or four times during the growing season. (See "Fertilizing" in Chapter One.) Make the first application in early spring. Withhold fertilizer during late fall and winter while plants are in the partially inactive dormant stage of their annual cycle.

Because many palms tolerate pot-bound roots, they do not need to be repotted as frequently as do many other house plants. When repotting palms, use only a slightly larger container for each successive repotting; increase the diameter of the container by only an inch or two.

Do not prune palms to control their size. Many cannot tolerate being cut and will not generate new fronds (leaves) if pruned. Large palms will eventually outgrow your home and will have to be discarded or given to a store or office that has room for the plants to continue to grow.

During the summer, move plants outdoors for a season of fresh air and to add the lushness of your palms to outdoor living areas which receive bright, indirect light. Avoid exposing palms to direct sunlight for prolonged periods. If vacations or work take you out of town for more than four or five days at a time, ask a friend or neighbor to water your palms while you are away.

Ponytail palm (*Beaucarnea recurvata*), also known as elephant-foot tree, is a striking plant. It is displayed here with chrysanthemums.

The butterfly palm (*Chrysalidocarpus lutescens*) is another good choice for dramatic indoor effect.

55

Palm Culture Guide

Latin Name	Common Name	Size	Adaptation	Light	Soil	Water	Rate of growth
Beaucarnea recurvata	Elephant-foot tree	10'-30'	Indoors, drought resistant; Outdoors, zone 10	Direct sun; 800-1000fc	Loamy	Partially dry between thorough waterings	Slow; eventually outgrows indoor location
Caryota mitis	Fishtail palm	to 10' or more	Indoors; Outdoors, zone 10	Bright indirect; 400-600fc	Loamy	Slightly moist at all times	Moderate; cannot be pruned to control size
Chamaedorea elegans (formerly Neanthe bella)	Parlor palm, Neanthe palm	12"-18"	Indoors, among easiest palms to grow	Moderate to low; 150-300fc	Loamy	Slightly moist at all times	Slow; growth rate controlled by potting small to restrict root growth; young plants good for terrariums
C. erumpens	Bamboo palm	to 10'	Indoors; Outdoors, zones 9-10	Bright indirect; 800-1000fc	Loamy		
Chamaerops humilis	European fan palm	4'-6'	Indoors; Outdoors, zones 9-10	Direct sun or bright indirect; 800-1000fc	Loamy	Moist at all times	Moderate
Chrysalidocarpus lutescens	Butterfly palm, Cane, Golden feather, Madagascar palm	5'-6'	Indoors; Outdoors, zone 10	Bright indirect or moderate; 400-600fc	Loamy	Moist at all times	Moderate; cannot be pruned to control size
Cycas revoluta (formerly C. inermis)	Sago palm	18"-24"	Indoors; Outdoors, zone 10	Bright indirect or moderate; 400-600fc	Loamy	Partially dry between thorough waterings	Slow to moderate
Cyperus alternifolius gracilis	Slender umbrella plant	12"-20"	Indoors; Outdoors, zone 10	Direct sun or bright indirect; 800-1000fc	Loamy; also grows in plain water	Wet at all times	Moderate
Howeia belmoreana (formerly Kentia belmoreana) H. fosteriana (formerly Kentia fosteriana)	Sentry palm, Curly palm, Kentia Palm, Paradise palm	to 10' or more	Indoors, among easiest palms to grow; Outdoors, zone 10	Bright indirect or moderate; 400-600fc	Loamy	Slightly moist at all times	Slow; plants tolerate cramped roots
Livistona chinensis	Chinese fountain palm, Chinese fan palm	to 10' or more	Indoors; Outdoors, zones 8-10	Bright indirect or moderate; 400-600fc	Loamy	Very moist at all times	Slow; eventually outgrows indoor location
Phoenix dactylifera	Date palm	to 10' or more	Indoors; Outdoors, zone 10	Direct sun or bright indirect; 800-1000fc	Loamy	Moist at all times	Moderate; eventually outgrows indoor location
P. roebelenii	Pigmy date palm, Miniature date palm	18"-24"	Indoors; Outdoors, zones 9-10	Bright indirect or moderate; 400-600fc	Loamy	Very moist at all times	Slow; can be used in terrariums, miniature gardens when young
Rhapis excelsa R. humilis	Lady palm, Slender lady palm	4'-6'	Indoors	Bright indirect or moderate; 400-600fc	Loamy	Very moist at all times	Slow to moderate
Syagrus weddeliana	Coco palm	6"-8"	Indoors; Outdoors, zone 10	Direct sun or bright indirect; 600-800fc	Loamy	Slightly moist at all times	Slow
Zamia floridana	Coontie	3'-4'	Indoors; Outdoors, zones 9-10	Direct sun, bright indirect, or medium; 600-800fc	Loamy	Partially dry between thorough waterings	Slow

Bromeliads

Some plants need no soil around their roots to prosper because their leaves can absorb moisture and nutrients directly from the air. Such plants are called *epiphytes*. The roots of epiphytes cling to trees, stones, or other supports that will allow them to "breathe."

Bromeliads, most of which are epiphytes, are spectacular plants. Many species bloom only once in their lives and then die, but the blooms are so dramatic and exquisite that they are well worth the wait. Foliage of bromeliads is unusually varied, and most that are cultivated in the home have spiny leaf edges arranged in cuplike rosettes to aid the plants in obtaining moisture from the atmos-

Some Favorite Bromeliads

Aechmea fasciata

Neoregelia carolinae

Aechmea angustifolia

Neoregelia carolinae tricolor

phere. Among the most familiar genera of bromeliads are *Aechmea, Billbergia, Cryptanthus,* and *Nidularium*.

Bromeliads are often expensive, but their long life and showy flowers make them worth their price.

Caring for Bromeliads

Most bromeliads like brightly lighted rooms, and thrive near windows that are not exposed to direct sun. If you summer your plants outdoors, a practice especially recommended for bromeliads, place them in open shade, such as that found under a tree. Bromeliads are often displayed hanging from trees as they do in their natural habitat. Bromeliads also respond well to artificial lighting. Provide at least 500 foot-candles for satisfactory results. (See "Lighting Needs" in Chapter One.)

Bromeliads thrive in a humid environment. Mist plants every day or use an electric humidifier. A humidifier accomplishes the dual purpose of providing moisture in the air as well as circulating it. Good circulation and ventilation plus high relative humidity are essential for success with bromeliads. If a humidifier is not available, you can raise the humidity around a plant by placing potted bromeliads on a shallow tray of pebbles filled nearly to the top with water.

Watering bromeliads is easy; keep the cuplike leaf rosettes filled with water. Water the roots only occasionally and then avoid overwatering.

Fertilize bromeliads monthly from February to early November, using a very mild liquid solution. Withhold fertilizer during the winter. (See "Fertilizing" in Chapter One.) Apply fertilizer to the rosettes as you would water.

During the summer, locate bromeliads outdoors where they will receive bright, indirect light but no direct sun.

Few insects attack bromeliads, but it is wise to always be on the lookout for scale insects and mealybugs. If you should detect either of these, pick them off by hand or wash them off with soapy water and an old toothbrush. If the infestation becomes rampant before you discover it, spray the plants with malathion or rotenone.

Propagating Bromeliads

Propagation of bromeliads is simple. Each plant produces offsets (baby plants) that grow at the base of the mother plant. These can be left attached to the mother plant for a display that will become increasingly spectacular as the offsets ma-

ture and bloom, or you can detach them and display them separately when the offsets are about one-third the size of the parent plant. With a sharp knife, remove the offset, cutting as close as possible to the mother plant. Trim excess growth from the cut end and remove withered leaves. Pot the offset in a sandy potting mix, or wrap the basal portion of the offset in moist sphagnum moss and display it on a wall or on a driftwood "bromeliad tree."

Many gardeners prefer to display their bromeliads on a piece of driftwood to give the impression of a tree. Wrap the roots of the bromeliads in sphagnum moss; then lodge the roots in a crack in the driftwood. You may want to further secure the plants to the driftwood with wire or nylon string.

Bromeliad Culture Guide

Latin Name	Common Name	Adaptation	Light	Soil	Water
Aechmea caudata A. chantinii A. fasciata	Aechmea	Indoors	Bright indirect; 800–1000fc	Sandy peat	Soil moist at all times; leaf cup filled with water
Ananas comosus variegatus A. nana	Pineapple Dwarf pineapple	Indoors Indoors	Direct sun; 1000–1200fc	Peaty loam	Soil moist at all times
Billbergia norrida tigrina B. leptopeda B. nutans B. pyramidalis	Billbergia	Indoors	Direct sun fall to spring; bright indirect in summer; 800–1000fc	Sandy peat	Soil moist at all times; leaf cup filled with water
Cryptanthus bivittatus C. fosteriana	Earth star, Crypthanthus	Indoors	Bright indirect; 800–1000fc	Peaty loam	Partially dry between thorough waterings
Dyckia fosteriana	Dyckia	Indoors	Direct sun or bright indirect; 800–1000fc	Peaty loam	Partially dry between thorough waterings
Guzmania lingulata G. momostachya	Guzmania	Indoors	Bright indirect; 800–1000fc	Peaty loam	Soil moist at all times; leaf cup filled with water
Nidularium fulgens N. innocentii striatum	Nidularium	Indoors	Bright indirect; 800–1000fc	Peaty loam	Soil moist at all times; leaf cup filled with water
Quesnelia humilis	Grecian vase plant, Quesnelia	Indoors	Bright indirect; 800–1000fc	Peaty loam	Soil moist at all times; leaf cup filled with water
Tillandsia cyanea	Tillandsia	Indoors	Bright indirect; 800–1000fc	Peaty loam	Soil moist at all times
Vriesia guttata V. splendens	Painted feather Flaming sword, Vriesia	Indoors	Bright indirect; 800–1000fc	Peaty loam	Soil moist at all times; leaf cup filled with water

The Easiest Orchids

The fascination of growing orchids as a hobby is becoming more popular with indoor gardeners everywhere. New methods of propagation have brought the cost of plants down in recent years, so growing orchids is no longer prohibitively expensive. While the controlled growing conditions of a greenhouse give a decided advantage, many orchids can be grown at home without special equipment or elaborate care.

Flowers range from nearly pinhead size to those as large as saucers. Some provide fragrance in addition to exotic beauty. Flowers may be produced in abundance on long pendant spikes or singly at the end of an erect stem. Predominant colors include lavender, pink, rose, red, yellow, and white. By selecting plants according to their season of bloom, you can have flowers almost any time of the year.

Orchids are of two basic growth habits: epiphytic and terrestrial. *Epiphytes*, in their native habitat, are attached to trees for support and receive nutrients from organic debris deposited at their roots by wind and rain. Most tropical orchids are epiphytes and must be kept dry during some periods of their growth cycle. *Terrestrial* orchids, on the other hand, grow with their roots in soil and need water throughout the year.

Orchid foliage is usually evergreen and is often tough and leathery. A few orchids have attractive foliage all year, but that of most species is not attractive when the plants are not in bloom.

Orchid plants grow in one of two ways: *monopodially* or *sympodially*. Those with the monopodial style of growth bear leaves in two rows on opposite sides of a central stem and continue to grow taller each year. The sympodial growth habit is the more common. New growth arises from the base of the plant each year, matures in one season, and produces flowers.

Orchids are often grouped into general categories according to the temperatures they prefer for best growth. Many orchids are native to New Guinea and Central and South America, but

Cymbidium orchids are the reward of this grower. The serious orchid fan will want to own a greenhouse sooner or later.

Cattleya orchid

60

Asia and Africa also contribute to the orchid population; few species can be found in frigid mountain or hot desert areas.

Caring for Orchids

Despite the fact that many orchids come from tropical or subtropical locations, the average winter home temperatures of 60° at night and 70° degrees during the day will suit a great many orchids. By grouping plants that prefer a cooler temperature near a window, and warmth-loving plants farther from the window, favorable conditions can often be simulated inside most homes.

Any kind of container with a hole for drainage can be used for orchids. Special slotted clay pots are preferred by many growers. If standard clay pots are used, drainage holes should be enlarged. Baskets of redwood or wire make good containers for some types of orchids. If plastic or glazed ceramic pots are used, care must be taken not to overwater the plants. The use of fir bark as a growing medium will help alleviate the drainage problem since it dries fairly rapidly.

Sun and light requirements vary considerably among the various species of orchids. Most thrive in filtered sunlight where the air circulates freely. A small oscillating fan is useful to keep the air moving.

An ideal growing medium for all orchids is difficult to find, but fir bark comes the closest of the materials commonly available. This medium is used by a great many orchid growers, although some still prefer osmunda fiber (the aerial roots of osmunda fern). Fir bark is sold in pieces graded according to size. It is easy to work with and, unlike osmunda, can be used either wet or dry when potting plants. Because fir bark deteriorates with age, however, most plants need to be repotted in fresh bark after about 18 months.

Although some orchids require a humidity level of 60% or higher, many plants respond favorably to indoor humidity which is between 30% and 40%. The purchase of an inexpensive hygrometer to measure humidity is a worthwhile investment. Hygrometers are often available at hardware stores. To increase the humidity around orchid plants, place the pots on a tray of wet gravel. Mist the air surrounding your plants with an atomizer, or you may want to install a portable humidifier.

There is no easy rule indicating how often to water your orchids. The size containers used will determine the frequency of watering. Large pots dry out slowly; wire baskets require more water than solid containers. The more heat used in your home, the more water plants need. Always use tepid water; a temperature of 60° to 70° is best.

Orchids should be fed regularly with a soluble orchid fertilizer during periods of active growth. During inactive periods and when light intensity is low, do not apply fertilizer. Orchids growing in fir bark will need more frequent applications of nitrogen fertilizer than plants growing in osmunda.

Laeliocattleya orchid

Orchids for Beginners

Many people know only the familiar purple or white cattleya orchid. This is surprising when you consider that the orchid family is the largest plant family known, comprising at least 25,000 species.

By careful selection, any interested grower can choose orchids that will tolerate the growing conditions he can provide. Orchid genera considered the easiest to grow and flower, even under adverse growing conditions, include many species and hybrids of *Phalaenopsis, Dendrobium, Epidendrum,* and *Vanda.*

Phalaenopsis. Plants in this genus are commonly known as moth or butterfly orchids. They are of a monopodial growth habit with broad, curving

Phalaenopsis orchid

leaves. Some plants develop all of the buds on the spike at about the same time; others open the basal flowers first, while the tip of the spike continues to form new buds. Frequently, when a flower spike is cut off just below the first flower, a secondary spike will develop on the old stalk. In this way plants will continue to bloom for many months of the year.

Dendrobium. The variation in this group of orchids is evident in its large number of species—more than 1,500. Some produce erect or arched sprays with five to twenty flowers, others have drooping sprays of a dozen to a hundred blooms, and still others bear clusters of flowers at each node for almost the entire length of the flower stalk.

Together with its hybrids *Dendrobium phalaenopsis* is now the most widely grown of all *Dendrobiums.* Lavender or white flowers appear in late fall in great profusion on canelike growth with many leaves. A healthy plant in a 6-inch pot can have a dozen or more sprays and over 100 flowers. *Dendrobiums* produce offsets which, when well rooted, can be snipped off the parent plant and potted by themselves.

Epidendrum. Small pastel flowers borne in great numbers are characteristic of members of this genus. They are one of the easiest groups of orchids to grow and one of the most prolific. The tall, reedlike growth of some species continously puts out aerial roots. It is a simple matter to start a new plant by taking a tip cutting with a few aerial roots and potting it.

Vanda. Their wide range of colors and the long life of the flowers make this group popular among orchid growers. These orchids are often used in hanging baskets outdoors in warm climates. *Vandas* grow upright in a monopodial growth habit and have many strap-shaped or pencillike leaves.

basal leaves that are leathery in appearance. Flowers are primarily white, pink, yellow, or multicolored, and may be 4 to 5 inches across. Individual flower spikes may bear from six to a dozen or more flowers that remain open on the plant for two months or longer.

The flower spike is tall and arched in most species and originates from the axils of the lower

Bulbs and Bulblike Plants

Few flowering plants respond to indoor culture better than bulbs. Some bulbs, such as amaryllis or canna, may be kept in containers for years at a time, requiring no more attention than the simplest house plants. They may be potted at any time of the year and forced into bloom after 8 to 10 weeks of proper cold storage.

Fragrance gardening is easier with bulbs than with any other group of flowering plants. The selection of fragrant, bulb-grown flowers is wide and can provide a succession of delightful scents throughout the year.

Soil for Container-Grown Bulbs

Bulbs already potted and ready to grow are available commercially, or you can purchase the bulbs separately and pot them in clay and plastic pots or in shallow bowls.

Potting media used in container bulb culture include coarse bulb fiber, vermiculite, and sharp sand (or perlite) or pebbles and water. Loamy garden soil is also a suitable medium.

Bulb fiber is a mixture of coarse peat, sand (or crushed shell), and powdered charcoal. Soak the fiber in a basin of water and squeeze it out. Fill a bowl or shallow pot almost to the top with fiber,

The brightly colored foliage of potted caladiums imports an almost festive air to this poolside patio.

The pert flowers and foliage of crocus make a delightful show planted in a small basket.

Tulips are superb bulbs for containers. Be sure they have had proper cold treatment before planting them.

for the successful growth of roots, foliage, and flowers. If you purchase inferior bulbs, the results may be disappointing.

Many bulbs need cold treatment before being planted in containers. Ask the nurseryman or retailer where you buy your bulbs if the bulbs are ready to force into bloom or if they need preplanting cold treatment. If cold treatment is required, store bulbs in the vegetable crisper of your refrigerator for about two months; then plant them.

Do not be afraid to crowd bulbs in container planting. When forcing large bulbs, such as narcissus and tulips, place three to five bulbs in a 7-inch pot or six to eight bulbs in a 10-inch pot. With very large bulbs, such as amaryllis, place one bulb in a 4-inch pot, three bulbs in an 8-inch pot, or five to six bulbs in a 10-inch pot.

To plant bulbs in an outdoor tub, place a piece of broken pottery over the drainage holes in the bottom of the container and cover this with a handful or two of coarse gravel. Add a 1-inch layer of charcoal, then fill the tub with a soil mix and place the bulbs just beneath the soil surface. Water thoroughly.

When planting bulbs in bowls or other shallow containers, fill the bottom with pebbles. Over this, add an equal volume of vermiculite, soil mix-

pressing the fiber down to leave a slight depression in the center. Place the first bulb in the center, and position the others around it so that the bulbs support each other. Bulb fiber is available at most retail garden supply stores.

Vermiculite and *perlite* are also common growing media for bulbs. Fill the pot nearly full with vermiculite; then soak with water, and allow the water to drain. Form a slight depression in the center and place the first bulb in it; then position other bulbs around the central bulb so that they support each other.

Pebbles and *water* is the simplest medium for forcing bulbs. Select a bowl or dish at least 3 inches deep and fill the bottom with a 1-inch layer of charcoal. Add to this about 1½ inches of clean ¾-inch pebbles. Add enough water to reach the bottoms of the bulbs. If you use a pot, plug the drainage hole in the bottom with a cork.

Always purchase top quality bulbs for forcing. The larger the bulb the larger the flowers. Stored within the bulbs are all the ingredients necessary

Grapehyacinth (*Muscari botryoides*) is an excellent candidate for container culture.

To pot bulbs, first place crockery and gravel in the bottom of the container to assure adequate drainage.

ture, or bulb fiber. Place bulbs in the container and fill in around them with more vermiculite or bulb fiber. Fill the container with water to the bottoms of the bulbs.

Caring for Bulbs

By far the simplest method of forcing a bulb into flower indoors during the winter months is to purchase a bulb already planted. All you need to do is give the bulb a warm temperature (60° to 65°), open light but no direct sun, and an adequate supply of water.

If bulbs used for forcing are to be used again, a light application of liquid plant food should be made every 2 weeks during the flowering period. When flowers fade, cut off flowering stems, but continue to water and feed. Keep the new top growth shaded from direct sunlight until it greens up. After the leaves yellow, withhold water and let the plant dry out. Repot in late fall or early winter and store the bulbs right in their pots for a two to three month rest period.

Some bulbs can be forced indoors only once; then they must be planted outside if another bloom season is expected. These include crocus, freesia, galanthus, gladiolus, hyacinth, lily, narcissus (including daffodils), spiderlily, sternbergia, and tulip.

Fill the pot ⅔ full with moisture-holding soil mix and place the bulbs in the pot so that they hold each other up. Water thoroughly.

Bulb Culture Guide

Latin Name	Common Names	Adaptation	Flower Color	Light	Water
Achimenes sp.	Achimenes	Indoors; Outdoors, zone 10	Red, pink, purple, blue, yellow, white	Filtered shade or bright indirect; 800–1000fc	Moist at all times
Agapanthus africanus	Lily-of-the-Nile, African lily	Indoors; Outdoors, zones 9–10	Purple, blue, white	Direct sun; 1000–1200fc No midday sun in summer	Constantly moist in growing season
Begonia x tuberhybrida	Tuberous begonia	Indoors; Outdoors, zone 10	Red, pink, orange, yellow, white	Bright indirect; 800–1000fc Direct sun in winter; 1000–1200fc	Constantly moist in growing season
Caladium bicolor	Caladium	Indoors; Outdoors, zones 7–10		Bright indirect to medium shade; 400–600fc	Constantly moist in growing season; withhold water in winter
Canna x generalis	Canna	Outdoors, zones 8–10	Red, pink, salmon, orange, yellow, white	Direct sun	Constantly moist in growing season
Clivia miniata	Kaffir lily, Clivia	Indoors; Outdoors, zones 8–10	Orange, yellow, white	Filtered shade or bright indirect; 800–1000fc	Constantly moist in growing season; slightly moist in winter
Crinum sp.	Crinum, Veld lily	Outdoors, zones 9–10	Red, pink, white	Filtered shade or direct sun; no midday direct sun	Constantly moist in growing season; partially dry in winter
Crocus sp.	Crocus	Outdoors, zones 5–9	Purple, blue, yellow, white	Direct sun or filtered shade	Slightly moist at all times
Cyclamen persicum giganteum	Cyclamen	Indoors; Outdoors, zones 5–9	Red, pink, white	Filtered shade or bright indirect; 800–1000fc	Constantly moist in growing season; partially dry in summer
Freesia x refracta	Freesia	Indoors; Outdoors, zones 9–10	Pink, purple, blue, yellow, white	Direct sun or bright indirect; 800–1000fc Partial shade when in bloom	Constantly moist in growing season; partially dry in fall and early winter

Bulb Culture Guide *(continued)*

Latin Name	Common Names	Adaptation	Flower Color	Light	Water
Hippeastrum sp.	Amaryllis	Indoors; Outdoors, zones 8–10	Red, pink, salmon, white	Direct sun, bright indirect when in bloom; 800–1000fc	Constantly moist in growing season; also grown in water
Hyacinthus sp.	Hyacinth	Indoors; Outdoors, zones 6–9	Red, pink, blue, yellow, white	Direct sun, bright indirect when in bloom; 800–1000fc	Constantly moist in growing season; also grown in water
Lilium longiflorum	Lily, Easterlily	Indoors; Outdoors, zones 4–9	Nearly all colors, including bi- and tricolored varieties	Bright indirect; 800–1000fc; direct sun after bloom	Constantly moist in growing season; slightly moist in late summer and fall
Muscari botryoides	Grape hyacinth	Indoors; Outdoors, zones 3–9	Pink, blue, white	Direct sun; 1000–1200fc	Constantly moist in growing season
Narcissus sp.	Daffodil, Jonquil, Narcissus	Indoors; Outdoors, zones 4–9	Yellow, white	Filtered sun or bright indirect; 800–1000fc	Constantly moist to wet in growing season; partially dry in summer
Sprekelia formosissima	Aztec lily	Indoors; Outdoors, zones 9–10	Red	Direct sun; 1000–1200fc	Constantly moist until foliage withers; withhold water in fall
Strelitzia reginae	Bird-of-paradise	Indoors; Outdoors, zone 10	Orange and blue combination	Direct sun; 1000–1200fc	Partially dry between thorough waterings
Tulipa sp.	Tulip	Indoors; Outdoors, zones 4–7	All colors except blue	Filtered sun or bright indirect; 800–1000fc	Constantly moist until foliage withers
Zantedeschia americana	Calla lily	Indoors; Outdoors, zone 10	Pink, yellow, white	Bright indirect but direct sun in morning; 800–1000fc	Constantly moist until foliage withers; withhold water in summer

Annuals and Perennials

Growing annual and perennial flowers in containers demands more time and care than growing them in the open ground. They require frequent watering and judicious grooming if you intend to display them in prominent places. Purchase soil mixture at the garden supply store, or make it yourself by mixing equal parts garden loam, sharp sand, and finely ground compost. Vermiculite or perlite may be substituted for sand; peat moss may be substituted for compost. Mix in ½ teaspoon of complete fertilizer per 6-inch pot.

Containers suited to growing annuals and perennials include pots, tubs, window boxes, cans, planters, and hanging baskets. Imagination and a good look around your house will turn up many containers that are suitable for growing annuals. Be sure the container has good drainage. If there are no holes near the base of the container, make two or three. Do not make drainage holes in the bottom of a container that will sit on a flat surface; drainage will be hampered. Instead, make holes in the sides near the base of the container.

Planting and Care of Annuals and Perennials

Spacing requirements are less stringent for container-grown plants than for the same plants growing in the ground. A 6- to 8-inch pot will hold three to five plants, whereas the same plants would require more room if planted outside. Sow seed directly in containers, or transplant commercially grown plants from flats. Transplants provide immediate color if the plants are already in bloom. Space requirements in the container are easier to gauge when using plants instead of seed.

Feed annuals and perennials monthly with complete fertilizer in liquid solution. Dissolve 2 tablespoons of fertilizer in 1 gallon of water. Make the first feeding about one month after planting, then once a month until the plants have finished blooming.

Feel the soil before watering. When the soil is somewhat dry and the plants begin to droop, add water. When water begins to seep through the drainage holes at the base, you have watered sufficiently. Do not overwater.

Marigolds enliven this patio.

Dianthus 'Orchid Lace' in a stationary planter.

Madagascar periwinkle (*Vinca rosea*) is a good choice for a hanging basket.

To prolong flower production on annuals and perennials, continually remove faded flowers. Discard annuals after all blooms have faded and the plants show signs of dying.

Perennials can be kept over from year to year in containers as long as they are repotted annually. Divide clumps when they become too large for their container, and pot the divisions to obtain additional plants. Potting and dividing are best done in spring. Perennials grown in containers may eventually become leggy and sparse. When this happens, take cuttings of healthy branches and root them in a mixture of equal parts sand and peat moss to form new plants. Then cut the leggy stems of the mother plant back to within 2 inches of the soil level.

Routine watering and fertilizing can cause crusting of excess salts on the surface of the soil. When this occurs, loosen the surface gently with an old fork or spoon, taking care to disturb plants and roots as little as possible, and scrape off the white crust. Replace lost soil with fresh soil.

Some plants make good companions for annuals and perennials in containers, especially in flower boxes. Try these in combination with your favorite annuals: asparagus fern, caladium, coleus, English ivy, geranium, and strawberries.

Flower Boxes

Flower boxes can be enjoyed from both inside and outside the home. If you are building your own flower box, use redwood, cypress, or wood pretreated to resist decay. Coat untreated wood with a wood preservative that is not toxic to plants, such as copper naphthenate. You may want to paint the outside of the box to complement the color of the house.

Build the box at least 10 inches wide and 8 inches deep. Use brass screws to hold the box together; nails are likely to pull out if boards warp. Reinforce the inside corners near the top with angle irons. Bore ½-inch drainage holes 6 inches apart in the bottom of the box.

Put up strong braces for reliable support when mounting the box on a wall. If the box is placed on the patio or deck, use blocks, bricks, or other firm support to raise the box for good air circulation and proper drainage.

To assure good drainage, spread 1 to 2 inches of gravel on the bottom of the box. Cover the gravel with a layer of sphagnum moss to prevent the soil from washing into the drainage layer. Fill the box with soil mix to within ½ inch of the top. Firm the soil, but do not pack it.

Place tall plants at the back, those of medium height in the center, and low-growers and cascading plants in front.

A mulch of ground bark or pine needles, about ½ inch deep, will conserve moisture. In very hot weather, boxes with a southern or southwestern exposure need watering in the morning and again during the middle of the afternoon. Never spray water on flowers or foliage when the sun is on the plants. In cool, cloudy weather, withhold water until the soil appears dry.

Many annuals can be grown in containers by sowing seed directly in pots of loamy soil. Dwarf varieties, such as these lilliput zinnias, are better suited to containers than tall-growing varieties.

Annual and Perennial Culture Guide

Latin Name	Common Names	Height	Type & Hardiness	Flower Color	Start from Seeds or Plants	Light
Ageratum houstonium	Ageratum (dwarf varieties)	6"–12"	Annual; frost tender	Pink, purple, blue, white	Seeds	Direct sun
Browallia speciosa major / B. viscosa compacta	Browallia Amethyst flower	1'–3'	Annual; frost tender	Blue	Seeds	Direct sun but no midday sun; also filtered shade
Campanula fragilis / C. isophylla	Bellflower, Campanula Italian bellflower	6"–3'	Perennial in zones 3–9	Pink, purple, blue, white	Seeds	Direct sun or filtered sun
Chrysanthemum sp.	Chrysanthemum, Mum	1'–4'	Perennial in zones 5–10	Red, pink, salmon, lavender, bronze, yellow, white	Plants	Direct sun
Senecio cruentis	Cineraria	12"–16"	Annual or perennial	Pink, purple, blue, white, mixed colors	Seeds	Partial shade; bright indirect
Dianthus sp.	Pinks	6"–12"	Annual; frost tender	Red, pink, white	Seeds	Direct sun
Felicia amelloides	Blue Marguerite, Blue daisy	1'–2'	Perennial in zones 9–10	Blue	Plants or seeds	Direct sun
Gazania longiscapa	Treasureflower, Gazania	Prostrate, 6"–18"	Perennial in zones 8–10	Red, pink, orange, yellow, lavender, cream	Plants or seeds	Direct sun
Impatiens sp. / I. balsamina / I. sultanii	Impatiens Balsam Sultana	1'–5' / 14"–24" / 12"–24"	Annual	Red, pink, lavender, white, combinations	Seeds	Partial shade; bright indirect
Ipomoea purpurea	Morningglory	Vine, to 10'	Annual	Red, purple, white	Seeds	Direct sun
Lobelia erinus	Lobelia	8"–10"	Annual	Blue, white, mixed colors	Plants or seeds	Direct sun or partial shade
Nicotiana alata grandiflora	Flowering tobacco, Nicotiana	1'–4'	Annual	Red, pink, salmon, purple, cream, white	Seeds	Direct sun
Pelargonium hortorum	Geranium	1'–3'	Perennial in zone 10	Red, pink, salmon, violet, white, black	Plants	Direct sun or partial shade
Petunia x hybrida	Petunia	8"–24"	Annual	Red, pink, salmon, purple, blue, cream, white; bi- and tricolors	Plants or seeds	Direct sun
Primula sp.	Primrose	8"–12"	Perennial in zones 4–10	Red, pink, blue, yellow, apricot, white	Plants or seeds	Partial shade
Reseda odorata	Mignonette	12"–18"	Annual	Bronze and white	Seeds	Direct sun or partial shade

Annual and Perennial Culture Guide (continued)

Latin Name	Common Names	Height	Type & Hardiness	Flower Color	Start from Seeds or Plants	Light
Tagetes patula	French marigold (dwarf varieties)	12″–16″	Annual	Red, orange, yellow, mahogony, bronze	Plants or seeds	Direct sun
Thunbergia alata	Blackeyedsusan vine, Clockvine	Trailing, 2′–5′	Perennial in zones 9–10	Orange, yellow, white; usually black or brown centers	Seeds	Direct sun
Tropaeolum majus	Nasturtium	12″–18″	Annual; can stand light frost	Red, pink, yellow, white	Seeds	Direct sun
Viola tricolor hortensis	Pansy	6″–10″	Annual; can stand light to medium frost	Red, purple, blue, yellow, bronze, white; bi- and tricolors	Plants	Direct sun or partial shade
Zinnia sp.	Zinnia (dwarf varieties)	6″–12″	Annual; frost tender	Red, pink, salmon, orange, gold, yellow, white	Seeds	Direct sun

Trees and Shrubs

Most trees and shrubs do not adapt well to indoor conditions. Homes are generally too dry and too warm, and such large plants are often difficult to move about as their temperature and dormancy requirements may demand. A number of shrubs and small trees, however, can be grown in containers on patios and decks, at entries, or other appropriate locations.

Some woody plants are either dwarfish by nature or are easily kept small by judicious pruning and grooming. These are well suited to container culture. The ideal tree or shrub for container culture is small, slow-growing, and adaptable to changes of location.

Be certain the container you select will accommodate the plant without cramping the roots. The container must have drainage holes in or near the bottom; few, if any, trees and shrubs will tolerate soggy soil.

Most plants grow well in a mix of equal parts garden loam, peat moss, and sand. Plants that prefer peaty soil should be potted in a mixture of 1 part loam, 1 part sand, and 2 parts peat moss, leaf mold, or compost. Plants that require light, dry soil should be potted in a mixture of 1 part loam, 1 part peat moss, and 2 parts sand or perlite. This mix is also suitable for plants that require especially good drainage. In general, improve drainage by increasing the proportion of sand, and improve water retention by increasing the content of peat.

Sterilize potting soil for best insurance against nematodes (destructive soil microorganisms) and soil-borne fungi which can cause disease problems. In addition, sterilization kills weed seed which may be present in garden soil or compost. See "Soils and Growing Media" in Chapter One for instructions on sterilizing soil.

Place gravel or broken crockery in the bottom of the container to assure good drainage; then fill the container with potting soil until the plant is at the correct height in the container. The top of the soil ball should be about ½ inch below the

The simplicity and elegance of these potted Japanese ligustrums (*L. japonicum*) add greenery to the brick and stucco without destroying the pleasing scale of the architectural features.

Many young shrubs make excellent house plants. Gold dust tree, or aucuba (*A. variegata*), with its yellow speckled foliage, makes a good show indoors or out.

72

Norfolk Island pine (*Araucaria heterophylla*) is one of the few needleleaf evergreens that can tolerate indoor conditions.

level of the rim to allow room for watering. Fill in around the root ball with additional potting soil; water thoroughly to allow for settling; then add more soil, if necessary, to bring the level of the soil to the correct height.

Caring for Trees and Shrubs

Allow the soil for most potted trees and shrubs to become partially dry between thorough waterings. Some, however, require more constantly even moisture. The chart at the end of this chapter suggests the most beneficial watering schedules for the plants discussed. Water slowly to allow the soil to absorb the water. As with other container plants, underwatering is less fatal than overwatering. A dry plant can wilt to warn you of its need for moisture; a waterlogged plant will usually die. Neither extreme is good for plants. Properly potted plants in porous, well-drained soil are not as susceptible to watering problems as carelessly pot-

ted plants. Learn to check plants regularly to see if they need watering, especially during hot dry weather. During dry spells and in dry climates, mist plants with a water spray bottle every 2 to 3 days.

Trees and shrubs have varying fertilizer needs. In general, most potted trees and shrubs can receive a light application of complete fertilizer twice a year. Make the first feeding in early spring as new growth begins; then feed again in the middle of the growing season, in June or early July. Slow-release fertilizers are best for most container-grown plants.

Do not overfertilize container-grown plants. Too much fertilizer can burn the roots and cause the plant to grow so quickly that it needs repotting more than once a year. Correct fertilizing of

Ligustrum (*L. japonicum*) in a ceramic container.

container plants consists of keeping them alive and well, but not growing too rapidly. Apply fertilizer according to manufacturer's directions.

Repotting and topdressing

Container plants may eventually become too large for their containers. Roots become matted and constricted and do not respond well to either water or fertilizer. Small plants can be moved to a larger container. Large plants, too big to repot, can be renewed by removing the top few inches of soil plus excess root growth, a process called "topdressing." Replace old top soil with fresh soil.

If the plant is young, or if you do not mind letting a mature plant grow a little larger, repot the plant in a larger container. Repotting should

Give weeping fig (*Ficus benjamina*) a large container and a sunny room with a high ceiling and it can become a splendid indoor tree.

be done on overcast days or at a time when the roots will not be exposed to direct sunlight.

If you do not want the plant to grow larger, you will need to remove some of the root system before repotting it in a similar sized container. Extensive trimming of roots is called "root pruning." Remove as much as one-third of the root system; then remove one-quarter of the top growth to compensate for the loss of roots. Try to remove branches that will open up the top of the plant, giving it a looser, more natural structure that promotes good air circulation among twigs and leaves. Keep root-pruned plants cool and well watered for two or three weeks after pruning roots.

Grooming

Because container-grown plants are displayed on patios, decks and other areas where you and your guests are likely to spend a great deal of time, you naturally want the plants to look their best. Keep old leaves and spent flowers removed. Do not hesitate to trim disproportionately long branches back to size. Annual pruning is desirable for many shrubs. The rain should keep the foliage clean, but if rainfall is sparse, it is a good idea to spray the foliage periodically with a fine strong stream from the hose. Hosing plants down not only removes dirt and grime but also helps prevent the buildup of insect populations.

A ½-inch layer of decorative mulch, such as pine bark nuggets, enhances the appearance of container-grown plants.

Winter protection

Because container plants are easily moved about to shelter them from the cold, tropical and subtropical plants can be grown outside their ordinary climate range. They will, however, require winter protection.

A few weeks before the first killing frost, move plants indoors. They will need a sunny or at least a bright location and cool temperatures. Daily misting will help satisfy humidity requirements. Do not locate plants near radiators or other heating outlets where they will dry out rapidly. Do not locate plants near outside doorways where they may be subjected to drafts and bruised by people passing by. Withhold fertilizer during the winter months, especially on deciduous plants.

Sun porches and enclosed decks are ideal winter locations because they provide light and yet keep the temperature cool. Ideal temperature range for over-wintering trees and shrubs is 45° to 50°.

Trees and Shrubs Culture Guide

Latin Name	Common Name	Size	Adaptation	Flower Color	Light	Soil	Water
Acer palmatum dissectum	Japanese maple	6'–10'	Outdoors, zones 5–9	Inconspicuous; red leaves throughout growing season	Partial shade	Peaty loam	Partially dry between thorough waterings
Araucaria heterophylla	Norfolk Island pine	4'–10'	Indoors; Outdoors, zone 10	Inconspicuous	Bright indirect to medium; 400–600fc	Sandy peat or sandy loam	Slightly moist at times
Aucuba japonica	Aucuba, gold dust tree	2'–4'	Indoors; Outdoors, zones 7–10	Inconspicuous	Bright indirect to medium; 400–600fc	Loamy	Slightly moist at all times
Bougainvillea spectabile	Bougainvillea	2'–6'	Indoors; Outdoors, zone 10	Red, pink, gold, yellow, white	Direct sun; 800–1200fc	Loamy	Partially dry between thorough waterings
Buxus sempervirens	Boxwood	1'–4'	Indoors; Outdoors, zones 5–10	Inconspicuous	Direct sun or bright indirect; 800–1000fc	Loamy	Slightly moist at all times
Camellia japonica	Common camellia	2'–4'	Indoors; Outdoors, zones 7–10	Red, pink, white, bi- and tricolors	Bright indirect; 800–1000fc	Peaty	Moist at all times
Carissa macrocarpa nana	Dwarf natal plum	1'–2'	Indoors; Outdoors, zones 9–10	White	Direct sun; 1000–1200fc	Sandy peat	Moist at all times
Citrus sp.	Orange, Calamondin orange, lemon, lime, grapefruit	1'–8'	Indoors; Outdoors, zones 9–10	White	Direct sun; 1000–1200fc	Loamy	Partially dry between thorough waterings
Coffea arabica	Coffee tree	2'–4'	Indoors; Outdoors, zone 10	White	Bright indirect 800–1000fc	Peaty loam	Moist at all times
Cotoneaster sp.	Cotoneaster	1'–1½', spreading	Indoors; Outdoors, zones 5–9	Yellow	Direct sun; 1000–1200fc	Loamy	Partially dry between thorough waterings
Daphne odora	Winter daphne	1'–2'	Indoors; Outdoors	Pink, white	Bright indirect; 800–1000fc	Peaty loam	Slightly moist at all times
Eriobotrya japonica	Loquat	4'–8'	Outdoors, zones 8–10	White	Direct sun or bright indirect	Loamy	Partially dry between thorough waterings
Euonymus fortunei gracilis	Wintercreeper	1'–2'	Indoors; hanging basket; Outdoors, zones 5–9	Inconspicuous	Medium; 400–600fc	Loamy	Slightly moist at all times
Feijoa sellowiana	Pineapple guava	2'–6'	Outdoors, tub, zones 8–10	Redish purple	Direct sun or bright indirect	Peaty loam	Slightly moist at all times
Ficus carica	Common fig	4'–8'	Indoors; Outdoors, zones 8–10	Inconspicuous	Direct sun or bright indirect; 800–1000fc	Loamy	Slightly moist at all times

Trees and Shrubs Culture Guide (continued)

Latin Name	Common Name	Size	Adaptation	Flower Color	Light	Soil	Water
Gardenia jasminoides G. radicans	Gardenia, cape jasmine Dwarf gardenia	1'–3' 6"–10", spreading	Indoors; Outdoors, zones 8–10	White	Direct sun or bright indirect; 800–1000fc	Peaty loam, well drained	Slightly moist at all times; use pebble tray to raise humidity
Hibiscus rosa-sinensis	Chinese hibiscus	2'–3'	Indoors; Outdoors, zones 9–10	Red, pink, orange, salmon, yellow, white	Direct sun; 1000–1200fc	Loamy	Slightly moist at all times
Hydrangea macrophylla	French hydrangea, bigleaf hydrangea	1½'–2½'	Indoors, first season; Transplant outdoors, zones 4–10, after bloom	Pink, blue, white	Direct sun inside, bright indirect; 800–1000fc	Loamy	Moist at all times indoors; slightly moist outdoors
Hypericum calycinum	Aaronsbeard, St. Johnswort	1'–3'	Outdoors, large tub, zones 6–9	Yellow	Direct sun or bright indirect	Peaty loam	Partially dry between thorough waterings
Ilex cornuta burfordii nana	Dwarf Chinese holly	1'–3'	Indoors; Outdoors, zones 7–10	Inconspicuous; red berries	Direct sun; 1000–1200fc	Peaty loam	Slightly moist at all times
Jacaranda acutifolia	Sharpleaf jacaranda	5'–10'	Indoors; Outdoors, zone 10	Blue	Direct sun	Sandy peat	Partially dry between thorough waterings
Jasminum mesnyi	Primrose jasmine	3'–10'	Indoors; Outdoors, zones 8–10	Yellow	Direct sun; 1000–1200fc	Loamy	Moist at all times
Lagerstroemia indica	Crape myrtle, dwarf myrtlette	2'–10'	Indoors; Outdoors, zones 8–10	Red, pink, purple, white	Direct sun; 1000–1200fc	Loamy	Partially dry between thorough waterings
Lantana camara L. montevidensis	Common lantana Trailing lantana	3'–4' 1'–2', spreading	Outdoors, zones 8–10; L. montevidensis zone 10	Red and yellow, L. camara; Pink, L. montevidensis	Direct sun	Loamy	Partially dry between thorough waterings
Ligustrum lucidum	Waxleaf ligustrum, glossy privet	4'–6'	Indoors; Outdoors, zones 8–10	White	Direct sun; 1000–1200fc	Loamy	Slightly moist at all times
Magnolia soulangiana M. stellata	Saucer magnolia Star magnolia	4'–10' 6'–10'	Outdoors, zones 4–9; M. stellata zones 5–9	White, pink inside; M. stellata, white	Direct sun, north; bright indirect, south	Peaty loam	Slightly moist at all times
Malus sp.	Dwarf apple, crabapple	6'–12'	Outdoors, zones 4–9	Red, pink, white	Direct sun	Loamy	Partially dry between thorough waterings
Musa nana	Dwarf banana	3'–4'	Indoors; Outdoors, zones 8–10	Redish purple	Direct sun; 1000–1200fc	Loamy	Moist at all times
Nandina domestica	Nandina, heavenly bamboo	3'–6'	Outdoors, zones 7–10	White	Direct sun or bright indirect	Peaty loam	Slightly moist at all times
Nerium oleander	Oleander	2'–6'	Outdoors, zones 8–10	Red, purple, yellow, white	Direct sun	Loamy	Partially dry between thorough waterings

Trees and Shrubs Culture Guide (continued)

Latin Name	Common Name	Size	Adaptation	Flower Color	Light	Soil	Water
Olea europa	Common olive	4'–8'	Outdoors, zones 9–10	White	Direct sun	Loamy or sandy, drained	Partially dry between thorough waterings
Osmanthus fragrans	Sweetolive	3'–4'	Indoors; Outdoors, zones 8–10	White	Direct sun; 1000–1200fc	Peaty loam	Slightly moist at all times
Pittosporum tobira P. tobira variegata	Pittosporum Variegated pittosporum	3'–7'	Indoors; Outdoors, zones 8–10	Inconspicuous	Direct sun or bright indirect; 800–1000fc	Loamy	Partially dry between thorough waterings
Podocarpus macrophyllus maki	Chinese podocarpus, yew podocarpus	4'–10'	Indoors; Outdoors, zones 7–10	Inconspicuous	Direct sun or bright indirect; 800–1000fc	Loamy	Slightly moist at all times
Prunus x hybrida	Peach, plum; dwarf forms	4'–8'	Outdoors, zones 4–9	Pink, white	Direct sun	Loamy	Partially dry between thorough waterings
Punica granatum nana	Dwarf pomegranate	3'–10', spreading	Indoors; Outdoors, zones 8–10	Red, yellow	Direct sun	Loamy	Partially dry between thorough waterings
Rhododendron sp.	Rhododendron, azalea	1'–8'	Indoors; Outdoors, zones 6–10	Red, pink, orange, white	Direct sun or bright indirect; 800–1000fc	Peaty loam	Slightly moist at all times
Rosa sp.	Miniature roses	6''–12''	Indoors; Outdoors, zones 7–10	Red, pink, yellow, white	Direct sun; 1000–1200fc	Loamy	Slightly moist at all times
Viburnum sp.	Arrowhead, wayfairing tree, viburnum	2'–6'	Indoors; Outdoors, zones 3–9	White	Direct sun or bright indirect; 800–1000fc	Loamy	Partially dry between thorough waterings

Bonsai for Beginners

The art of growing miniature trees in containers originated in ancient China. In the 13th century bonsai culture spread to Japan where it so captured the fancy of the Japanese people that within less than a century, most of the naturally dwarfed trees growing in the Japanese countryside had been gathered. When bonsai specimens became hard to find growing in the wild, collectors began to create bonsai trees from dwarfable cultivated plants, shaping and training them to give the illusion of advanced age and natural, rugged character.

American bonsai growers are freer in choice of plant material and style than their Oriental predecessors who, over a period of nearly 2,000 years, developed in bonsai culture an increasingly rigid and formalized horticultural art. Amateur bonsai enthusiasts in the West have no ethnic roots in the mystical Zen and Taoist traditions, which became an important part of the training of bonsai

Japanese black pine (*Pinus thunbergii*) is a popular subject for bonsai culture.

Many species of juniper make superb bonsai. Pictured here is *Juniperus virginiana*.

This intriguing juniper bonsai is grown on a piece of driftwood to create the illusion of an aged trunk.

plants. As a consequence, new methods of shaping and training specimens have, at the same time, freed the modern grower from many culturally related restrictions, but also lost for him a portion of the Oriental mysticism that is so much a part of this fascinating hobby. In this chapter, the major concern will be with the mechanics of bonsai; that is, the selection, training, and care of bonsai, designed for the beginning bonsai student.

Bonsai Styles

The fine classical styles of bonsai are *formal upright*, *informal upright*, *slanting*, *cascade*, and *semicascade*. To start with, a single trunk specimen is recommended. Decide which style best suits the plant you have chosen.

Formal upright. This is the easiest style since it involves no training to speak of. Upon pruning the plant to the desired shape, it becomes a displayable bonsai. Form may be conical or rounded. The lowest branch extends a little farther from the trunk than the others. Oval and rectangular containers best complement the formal upright style.

The formal upright style is the simplest bonsai style. Main characteristics of this style include a straight trunk and bottom branch that is slightly lower and longer than its opposite higher branch.

Informal upright. The major difference between this style and the formal upright is the straightness of the main stem. In the informal upright style, the main stem bends slightly to the front, giving an appearance of motion. Nursery plants are often naturally slanted and suited to this style. If you choose a vertical tree and want to prune it to this style, simply tilt the plant when you pot it. If the natural slant of the tree is not enough, attach

wires to increase the slant of the trunk. Trim the branches and foliage so that they are scaled to the size of the tree. Oval and rectangular containers enhance this style.

The informal upright style is characterized by a trunk that leans slightly to the front.

Slanting style. In this style, the trunk slants at a more acute angle than in the informal upright style, and the lowest branch spreads in a direction opposite to that in which the tree slants. The lowest branches are arranged in groups of three, starting about one-third of the way up the trunk. Found in the wild, trees that have been forced by the wind to lean acutely are easy to train to this style. The angle of the slanting is between that of the upright and cascade styles. Square or round containers are best for plants trained to the slanting style.

The slanting style resembles the informal upright style except that in the slanting style, the trunk is bent to a more acute angle.

Cascade style. Traditionally, the tree starts with an upward growth pattern, then turns downward to reach a point below the bottom of the container. Place cascading bonsai on the edge of a shelf or table so that it can cascade unhampered. In this style, the majority of the foliage is below the level of the soil surface to resemble a tree which, in nature, would be growing down the face of an embankment. This is a more exacting style and takes a little longer than when training a plant to the previous styles. Choose a low-growing, spreading species for this style rather than a naturally upright tree that would have to be forced into an unnatural form. Bend the tree forward so that one back branch is vertical and the side branches appear to fall naturally. Use a round or hexagonal container for plants that are trained to cascade.

Semicascade style. The trunk is allowed to grow straight for a distance (though not necessarily upright), then is cascaded downward, but at a less abrupt angle than in the cascade style. The semicascade style should allow the branches to reach a point level with or higher than the bottom of the container, but not higher than the soil surface.

When planting any bonsai, keep the overall theme in mind. Upright trees should look stable in their containers, whereas slanted and cascading bonsai often have portions of their roots exposed

The cascade style, like the semicascade style, calls to mind a mountainside planting. However, the slope of the trunk is more acute and can extend below the container. Prostrate plants, such as creeping junipers, lend themselves to the cascade and semicascade styles. Round containers are most often used for the two cascading styles.

to suggest the way that plants grow naturally on rocky mountain summits.

Decide firmly on a style at the outset. Once the plant has started growing in the style selected, it could be injured by changing the wires you may have attached to brace the plant in the desired form.

The semicascade style is reminiscent of the windswept trees found on an exposed mountainside. In this style, however, the trunk does not bend lower than the bottom of the container.

Obtaining Plants

A good bonsai specimen should possess a harmonious arrangement of branches. The branches must not look lopsided or top heavy, nor should they be precisely opposite each other. Looking directly down on the plant from above, there should be no unsightly gaps. The upper branches should not overshadow the lower ones.

You can create your own bonsai with cuttings from nursery stock, from naturally dwarfed trees growing near the summits of wooded mountains, or from seedling plants. The serious bonsai grower may want to import plants from Japan. The best time to have plants shipped is during the dormant season (November to February for most plants), because upon entering the United States, the plants are subjected to severe fumigation to prevent the entry of insects and plant diseases. Plants can best tolerate such fumigation when they are dormant. It is best to check with the United States Department of Agriculture before ordering plants to be certain that plants you want to order are not prohibited from entry into this country.

Training nursery plants

The best method for the beginner is to purchase a container-grown plant from the nursery and to dwarf it gradually for bonsai culture. Because these plants have been growing in containers, their roots are already accustomed to cramped conditions and are therefore over the first hurdle in bonsai culture. Buy only young, healthy plants that are well rooted and well branched. Only a sturdy plant will endure the severe initial pruning it must endure. Make sure the foliage is full enough from all sides to be shaped into an interesting bonsai.

The process of dwarfing consists of gradually pruning the top and roots of the plant to balance with one another until the plant and all of its parts are smaller. It is important to cut back roots as well as top growth in the initial pruning; to prune one without pruning the other could result in the death of the plant. The type of training style you decide upon will determine how much top growth to remove. Then, cut roots back a proportionate amount, and pot the plant in a slightly smaller container than the one in which it grew at the nursery. Each year remove a little more top growth and roots until the plant is scaled down to bonsai dimensions.

The time-tested plants that continue to be favorites for bonsai culture include the following:

Sargent juniper (*Juniperus chinensis sargentii*)
Japanese black pine (*Pinus thunbergii*)
Japanese wisteria (*Wisteria floribunda*)
Flowering cherry (*Prunus subhirtella*)
Japanese zelkova (*Zelkova serrata*)

Beginners will probably have the best luck (and fewest disappointments) with these plants:

Scarlet firethorn (*Pyracantha coccinea*)
Small-leaved cotoneaster (*Cotoneaster microphylla*)
Dwarf pomegranate (*Punica granatum nana*)

In the United States, many gardeners have applied bonsai pruning and training techniques to some common house plants, thereby creating an "indoor bonsai" culture with plants that can be kept indoors most of the year. True bonsai should not be brought indoors for more than a few hours at a time. The following make handsome bonsai specimens for indoors:

Balfour aralia (*Polyscias balfouriana*)
Boxwood (*Buxus* sp.)
Dwarf gardenia (*Gardenia jasminoides 'Radicans'*)
Citrus (*Citrus sp.*)
Arizona cypress (*Cupressus arizonica*)
Monterey cypress (*Cupressus macrocarpa*)
Cooper's Chinese hibiscus (*Hibiscus rosa-sinensis cooperi*)
Miniature holly (*Malpighia coccigera*)
Sharpleaved Jacaranda (*Jacaranda acutifolia*)
Jade (*Crassula* sp.)
India laurel (*Ficus retusa*)
True myrtle (*Myrtus communis*)
Orchid tree, Buddhist bauhinia (*Bauhinia variegata*)
Common olive (*Olea europaea*)
California pepper tree (*Schinus molle*)
Chinese pistachio (*Pistacia chinensis*)
Natal plum (*Carissa grandiflora*)
Royal poinciana (*Delonix regia*)
Dwarf pomegranate (*Punica granatum nana*)

Cuttings

Hardwood and softwood cuttings of woody plants can be rooted and trained as bonsai. Small-leaved shrubs such as azalea, forsythia, pussywillow, and juniper lend themselves particularly well to propagation from cuttings and to bonsai culture. Take softwood cuttings during the early part of the growing season, and root them in a mixture of equal parts sand and peat moss. Cuttings should be 3 to 6 inches long with as many healthy growth buds as possible. Remove lower leaves and insert cuttings 2 inches deep in the medium. Cover the pots or flats with plastic, or place plastic bags over each cutting, or cover the entire flat with a large sheet of polyethylene or glass. Locate the cuttings in filtered shade and keep the soil slightly moist. After cuttings have formed roots (1 to 4 months, depending on the species), plant them in the ground or in training pots for a year until they are ready for more decorative containers.

Collecting specimens in the wild

The time of year for collecting bonsai from the wild is early spring, just before their buds begin to open. A dwarfed tree is distinguishable from a small, young shoot by the branching habit; the older the tree, the more elaborate the framework of branches. Often, naturally stunted trees already appear twisted and aged. The most desirable naturally dwarfed trees are usually in the range of 6 inches to 30 inches. The larger the tree, however, the greater the difficulties in transplanting.

The best places to look for bonsai trees are exposed, rocky ledges which have patches of grass and other vegetation, including trees of varying sizes. The exposure, not necessarily the height of the mountain, will determine the likelihood of finding stunted trees. Rockiness is another factor. One of the reasons trees may become dwarfed is that the grass cover over the rock is so shallow that the roots of the tree have no room in which to grow.

Other elements can also stunt a tree. Because the roots are in shallow soil, the plant may not grow very tall without being blown away by the wind. If sunlight and moisture requirements are met, the tree may thrive and be perfectly healthy but simply not be very tall.

Many dwarfed mountainside trees grow out of cracks in the rocks and their roots are so firmly wedged into the rock that it is impossible to remove them without severe injury to the plant. These should be left where they are.

A number of species well suited to bonsai culture can be found in the wild. Among the most common are maple, box elder, huckleberry, beech, azalea, dogwood, cedar, elm, cypress, juniper, persimmon, and a number of oaks and pines.

Find an appealing specimen growing in loose turf. Probing with your fingers, you should be able to trace the main roots 6 to 10 inches into the ground. For the trees to survive, it is important to get a goodly portion of the root system. Try to retain as much of the attached soil as possible. The plant's native medium will help the roots adapt to new soil. To carry small specimens, fill the bottom of a sandwich bag with crumbly soil to cushion the roots. Place the roots in the bag and fill in around them with additional soil, pine needles, rotted leaves, or other humus material.

The trees must spend a year planted in an outdoor garden to help them gradually adjust to their new environment. Plant them in full sun as borders for walks or flower and vegetable gardens. They must be in rich, well-drained soil. After 10 to 15 months, they can be transplanted into containers.

Potting and Pruning Bonsai

At the end of the first year, transplant the tree from the ground or from its training pot into a more decorative pot suited to the dimensions of the plant. Trim the roots if necessary, but try to retain some of the original soil. Prune the taproot at potting time, prune it again after the second year, and cut it short at the end of the third year. Prune only slightly the smaller new roots at the base of the taproot.

A loamy potting soil, as is used for most house plants, is also satisfactory for most bonsai. Mix equal parts of garden loam, peat moss, and sand or perlite. Finely ground compost is a viable substitute for peat moss. Such a potting mixture provides fast drainage and enough substance to anchor the plant's roots.

Bonsai enthusiasts frequently find that appropriate containers are difficult to obtain. Because the container must also be in proportion to the plant and its parts, the relationship of container to plant in bonsai culture is often likened to that of the frame to a picture.

The container must remain secondary to the plant in color, form, and design so as not to compete with the plant. Shallow, traylike containers are ideal; they create a horizontal ground line suggesting a bit of landscape and making them suitable for many plant materials. The classic proportion often cited is 80% of the total height should be plant and 20% container. Variation on these proportions are sometimes necessary to accommodate broader or taller plants.

Keeping in mind the proportion requirements of bonsai plants makes it less difficult to find suitable containers or to adapt commonplace market items. Shallow containers made for flower arrangements may sometimes be adapted by providing holes for drainage.

Shaping and Training Bonsai

Decide which sides of the plant are front, back, and sides, and examine the roots that will govern the growth of each side. After deciding which style fits your tree, shape the plant by pruning, nipping and wiring. Number 10 wire will hold larger stems and branches.

Wire evergreen trees only when they are dormant (winter), and wire deciduous trees during their growing season (March to November) to minimize damage and shock to the plants. Withhold water the day before wiring a tree to make the tree more flexible.

Begin wiring and shaping at the bottom of the tree, and work upward. Anchor the low end of the wire in the soil before you begin winding. Wind the wire around those branches to be trained. Wire from the trunk to the main branch. Keep the turns about ¼ inch apart, and spiral upward at a 45 degree angle. Do not wire too tightly, and be careful not to damage leaves or stems. One length of wire can serve to bend 2 branches if the center of the wire is wrapped around the trunk. As you coil the wire around the trunk and branches of a tree, bend it gradually to the form you want them to take. Once a plant is wired, bend it a little more to the intended incline.

Caring for Bonsai

Although bonsai may be brought indoors for brief display, most bonsai must remain outside. During the growing season, locate plants where they will receive 3 to 5 hours of direct sunlight each day. Provide afternoon shade. Screening may be required to protect plants if you live in an area where drying winds are prevalent. During the winter, store plants in a cool greenhouse or in a cold frame. If the winter temperature in your area does not drop below 28°, the protection of a cold frame will be unnecessary.

During the growing season, water plants daily.

Bonsai tools (clockwise from bottom) include a chopstick for tamping soil, concave cutters, wire cutter, scissors, pruning shears, fishing line, hair pins, copper wire, tweezers, manicure scissors, and pastry brush. All are common materials except for the concave cutters which are made exclusively for bonsai culture.

How to Train a Bonsai

Chinese juniper selected for training as a bonsai.

Remove the plant from its nursery container and prune the roots to fit the bonsai container.

After deciding upon a shape for your bonsai, remove unwanted branches and twigs with scissors.

Place the plant in its container, and firm soil around the roots with a chopstick or other blunt instrument; then water gently but thoroughly, taking care not to disturb the soil.

Wrap the main branches with copper wire, then bend them in the desired direction. If the trunk is to be bent, wire it, too.

The finished bonsai.

Soil in shallow pots exposed to drying sun and air will lose moisture far more rapidly than most house plants indoors in deep containers. In midfall, begin to reduce watering as the plant enters its dormant period.

Fertilize bonsai monthly from early March to early November. Use a common house plant fertilizer such as fish emulsion, or use a mild solution of soluble fertilizer in water. Fertilize sparingly, just enough for plants to maintain a healthy level of nutrients, but do not overfertilize bonsai as this may stimulate unwanted growth. In bonsai culture, the goal is a small plant, not a big one.

Repotting becomes necessary if soil insects damage the plant, if the soil is in poor condition, or if the container breaks. The health of a bonsai depends largely on the care taken to change soil and to retain surface roots. Surface roots are a sign of a healthy bonsai, but if left to grow, the surface roots can mat the surface, hindering the penetration of air and water to the main roots. Periodically, thin out the surface roots, and cut back the main roots. Slow growers will need repotting no more frequently than once every three to five years. Vigorous plants should be repotted each year; in a few cases, twice a year.

The best time to repot is in early spring when the first new buds appear. Do not repot bonsai in winter (when roots are dormant and unable to establish themselves) or in late spring and summer when the leaves have only recently opened and are still tender.

Displaying Bonsai

Bonsai should be brought indoors for only a few hours or days at a time. Before bringing plants indoors for display, water them well and let them drain. Wipe the container clean. Bonsai are effective on a raised stand in front of a plain wall. A small Japanese screen, available from an Oriental decor store, is a fine background for indoor bonsai displays.

Outdoors, display bonsai specimens on the deck or patio. Group small plants together on a shaded shelf or stand. Plants in large containers are most effective displayed alone.

The serene elegance of bonsai trees creates an atmosphere of quiet and contemplation on this patio.

85

Vegetables and Herbs

Growing vegetables in containers is not difficult if you provide a sunny location for your plants and give them the daily attention they will require. Decks, patios, walkways, and other areas with limited space make excellent locations for container vegetable gardens. In fact, the more limited the area, the more effective the plants become as ornamentals. Ornamental value and interest will have to be the primary motives for raising a container vegetable garden, and, of course, a few delicious vegetables. But do not plan to fill your freezer.

Not all vegetables lend themselves well to container gardening. Corn is impractical (successful pollination requires a substantial planting) as are pumpkins and watermelons. But eggplant, peppers, cherry tomatoes, cucumbers, and many others perform quite well in the proper container in the right place.

In general, select plants of a compact growing habit for container culture. This is not meant to eliminate tall plants such as okra, which is a

superb container plant grown singly in a pot or massed in a large tub.

Containers and Soil for Vegetables

Your selection of vegetable plants will depend largely on the containers you plan to use. The most commonly available containers are planters, boxes, and large pots. These are suitable for a number of vegetable plants. The most versatile container, however, is a trough-style planter. Nearly anything that is grown as a row crop in the garden will thrive in such a container. A window box is excellent for English peas, bush beans, peppers, eggplant, or ornamental kale.

Of limited use, but unlimited appeal, is the hanging container. Not many vegetable plants are well suited to hanging baskets, but climbing vines such as pole beans and blackeyed peas can be grown in large containers and trained to cascade. English peas are a good choice for a simple hanging basket. Plant a few nasturtiums or sweetpeas with them to add a few blooms to the basket.

Tomatoes, pole beans, and other climbers can be grown in troughs or tubs if support is provided. Trellises are the most attractive means of support and can be fashioned to train plants to appealing forms.

The following suggestions will help you to select the right container for the plants.

Trough or Window Box

Beets	Eggplant
Broccoli	English peas
Brussels sprouts	Garlic
Bush Beans	Herbs
Cabbage	Kohlrabi
Carrots	Lettuce
Cauliflower	Mustard
Celery	Onions
Collards	Turnip greens

Turnips

Trough with trellis

Black-eyed peas	Pinto beans
Cucumbers	Polebeans

Tomatoes

The container vegetable garden can be as attractive as it is productive.

Pot

Brussels sprouts	Herbs
Cabbage	Lettuce (leaf)
Chard	Okra
Eggplant	Onions
Garlic	Peppers
	Tomato

Hanging basket

Cherry tomato	Herbs
English peas, snow peas	Pickling cucumbers
	Sweet potato

Tub

Asparagus	Combinations
Beets	Okra
Carrots	Squash
	Tomatoes

Containers for plants must have drainage holes either in the bottom or in the sides near the base. Fill the bottom of the container with 1 inch of gravel or charcoal, and add 1 inch of sphagnum moss or other organic matter on top of the gravel. Fill to within 1 inch of the top of the container with soil mix. Sow seed at the depth recommended on the seed packet, and water the planted container thoroughly.

Most vegetables will grow well in a mixture of equal parts garden loam, sand (or perlite), and peat moss. Finely ground compost, leaf mold, and rotted sawdust are excellent alternatives to peat moss. Such a mixture retains moisture and, at the same time, permits excess moisture to drain. Packaged potting soil is available at garden supply centers. The greatest advantage of packaged mixes

A sunny balcony, deck, patio, or porch can provide good locations for a container vegetable garden.

is that the soil has been sterilized. To sterilize your own soil mix, see "Soils and Growing Media" in Chapter One.

Caring for the Container Vegetable Garden

Porches, decks, patios, balconies, steps, and other sunny, prominent places are good locations for container plants. Primary considerations in locating plants include light and exposure to heavy rain or drying winds. Although vegetable plants in the open ground prefer full sun, container-grown plants should receive filtered sun. In full sun the soil can dry quickly, leaving plants susceptible to sunscorch. Mulch with 2 to 3 inches of ground bark to help conserve soil moisture. Full sun for part of the day, especially in the morning, will benefit most container-grown vegetables, but do not expose them to midday sun during the summer.

Watering

Water will evaporate from containers more quickly on hot, sunny days than on cloudy days. Check plants daily, and learn to gauge watering needs by the appearance of the plants and by feeling the soil. A watering can is best for irrigating container gardens; a hose may wash soil away from roots. On hot, dry days mist the foliage with a fine spray from the garden hose.

Moisture will evaporate from hanging containers faster than from containers on the ground. Check hanging baskets daily to see if they need water.

Fertilizing

Liquid concentrates, such as house plant fertilizers, are excellent for use on container-grown vegetables. Other suitable fertilizers include cottonseed meal and dehydrated manures. Liquid fertilizers are convenient to store and easy to apply. You can make your own liquid solution if you purchase water-soluble fertilizer. Be sure to specify to the retailer that you intend to make such a liquid fertilizer; then mix the solution according to label directions.

Apply liquid fertilizer in mild solution every other week. Apply cottonseed meal and manure once a month. For most plants, 1 teaspoon per plant per month will suffice.

Insect and disease control

All the insects that attack vegetables in the open ground can also attack container vegetables.

Control is easier in the container garden because there are fewer plants and because it is possible to quarantine infested plants.

Picking the insects off the plants by hand is the best method of insect control in a container garden, unless you are squeamish. A good spraying with a garden or sink hose will also remove insects.

Several insecticides are also useful. (See Chapter Fifteen, Problems in Container Gardens.) Rotenone, Sevin, and malathion will control most insect problems in a container vegetable garden.

Soil-borne fungus diseases and nematodes can be averted by using sterilized potting soil. Air-borne fungi can be controlled by using a general fungicide, such as Captan. (See Chapter Fifteen, Problems in Container Gardens.)

Herb Gardens in Containers

Herbs are regaining a place of importance among container gardeners. Their many uses in both cooking and potpourri make them popular items. In addition, the pleasantly scented leaves of a great many herbs increase their value and interest.

Herbs are hearty container plants, and, best of all, they are easy to grow. Like any plant, they require water, sun, and a growing medium. Herbs do best in a slightly alkaline soil (pH 7.0 or above), although they will grow in rich, slightly acid soils (pH less than 7). But under acid conditions, the plants will produce large leaves and lose their compact appearance. If the soil is too acid, add ground limestone to correct the situation.

There are many different herbs to choose from. (See chart.) Some are annuals, completing their life cycle in one year. Others are perennials that live from year to year, depending on the care given them. A few are biennial, having a two-year life cycle.

Herbs lend themselves to container culture, particularly the perennials. They can be grown in hanging baskets and pots in sunny locations.

Kitchen windowsills that receive plenty of sunlight are ideal for small 4- to 6-inch pots of herbs.

One desirable characteristic of herbs is their compact growth, which results from cutting and harvesting. You can start enjoying your crop as soon as the plants become established. Some are used freshly cut; others can be dried and stored in bottles, or packaged and kept in the freezer.

Most herbs are classified by botanists into either the mint, parsley, aster, or lily family.

Mint. Plants of the mint family have square

Many common herbs can be grown from seed. For an "instant" garden, however, buy started plants. Top row (left to right): comfrey, lemon balm, and wormwood. Bottom: southernwood, pennyrod, and sage.

stems with opposite aromatic leaves. Flowers are borne in clusters at the base of the uppermost leaves or in terminal spikes. Herbs in this family include the mints, thyme, marjoram, savory, lemon balm, sage, and rosemary.

Parsley. Herbs of the parsley family have small flowers formed in umbels at the tops of the hollow stems. Leaves are alternate and finely divided. This family includes anise, coriander, chervil, dill, fennel, lovage, and parsley.

Aster. Plants in the large aster family are recognized by their flowers. They are borne in composite heads like the daisy and sunflower. Only a few herbs, such as tarragon, belong to this family.

Lily. The lily family is composed chiefly of herbs with a bulbous or enlarged root system and annual stems. Leaves are generally slender, either flat or tubular, with veins running lengthwise. Herbs in this group are chives, garlic, leek, and onion.

Containers for herbs

A number of containers are suitable for indoor herb gardens. Pots (both clay and plastic), boxes, flats, strawberry jars, and hanging baskets all make excellent herb containers. In addition, window boxes, floor planters, and trays are often used for herb gardens. Small containers are, of course, more mobile and can easily be moved outdoors or onto porches and decks during the summer. You may plant only one kind of herb in each container, or plant several in a single container, placing the taller ones in the center, then medium-size plants around these, and dwarf plants or drooping plants around the outside of the container.

Whatever kind of container you select, be certain that the container has adequate drainage.

Herb Culture Guide

Herb (a)* (b) (c)	Planting Season	Propagation	Growth Pattern	Culinary Use	Part Used	Ornamental Use	Light Requirements	Harvest
Anise (a)	Spring	Seeds	1½'–2' upright	Seasoning or garnish	Leaves, seeds	Poor	Full sun	Leaves, as needed; seeds, when ripe
Basil (a)	Spring	Seeds	1½' upright	Seasoning	Leaves	Garden color	Full sun	As needed
Borage (a)	Spring	Seeds	2'–3' upright	Cucumberlike flavor in iced drinks	Flowers, leaves	Garden color	Full sun	Blossoms used as they open; leaves as needed
Caraway (b)	Fall	Seeds	2½' upright irregular	Seasoning	Seeds	Poor	Full sun	When ripe
Chervil (a)	Early spring	Seeds	Up to 2' compact	Seasoning and garnish	Leaves	Garden color	Semishade	As needed
Chives (p)	Spring	Seeds or division	10" in clumps	Onion flavor	Leaves	Border plants	Full sun	As needed
Costmary (p)	Spring	Seeds or division	4'–5' clumps	Seasoning	Leaves	Poor	Full sun	As needed or dried
Cumin (a)	Spring	Seeds	1' upright	Seasoning	Seeds	Poor	Full sun	Cut and dry plants in fall; thresh and clean seeds, and store in bags
Dill (a)	Spring	Seeds	2'–3' upright	Seasoning, especially with pickles	Seeds, leaves	Garden color	Semishade	Seeds, when ripe; leaves, as flowers open
Garlic (p)	Spring	Sets	2' upright	Seasoning	Bulbs	Poor	Full sun	Dig and dry mature bulbs
Ginger (p)	Spring	Root division	2' upright	Condiment	Rhizome	Good	Partial shade	Dig and dry rhizomes in the fall
Lavender (p)	Spring	Seeds or cuttings	1½'–3' upright		Flowers	Small varieties as border plants	Full sun	When first flowers open (use flowers for fragrance)
Lemon Balm (p)	Spring	Seeds or division	2' irregular spreading	Imparts lemony flavor to tea and other cool drinks	Leaves, sprigs	Poor	Full sun	As needed or dried
Mint (p)	Spring	Division or cuttings	2'–3' upright	Leaves used for tea and flavoring	Leaves	Poor	Full sun	Fresh, use anytime; dry, cut and dry just as flowering begins
Oregano (p)	Spring	Division	2½' spreading	Flavoring	Leaves	Poor	Full sun	Cut plants and dry in well-ventilated shade. Remove leaves when dry

Herb Culture Guide (continued)

(a)* Herb (b) (c)	Planting Season	Propagation	Growth Pattern	Culinary Use	Part Used	Ornamental Use	Light Requirements	Harvest
Parsley (b)	Early spring	Seeds	1½' upright	Seasoning or garnish	Leaves	Garden color, edging	Full sun	As needed, or dry at 150 degrees until crisp
Rosemary (b)	Fall	Plants, cuttings, seeds	3'–6' irregular	Seasoning	Leaves	Hedge, specimen plant	Full sun	As needed, or dry at 150 degrees
Sage (p)	Spring, fall	Seeds or cuttings	2' and sprawling regular	Seasoning	Leaves	Fair	Full sun	Cut 5" of leafy top and hang in shade to dry
Sesame (a)	Spring	Seeds	2'–3' upright	Condiment for bakery goods, confections, candies	Seeds	Good	Full sun	Harvest and dry the mature seeds. Store in airtight container
Summer Savory (a)	Spring	Seeds	18" upright	Condiment with meats and vegetables	Leaves	Poor	Full sun	Cut leaves at budding time and dry in airy, shaded place until crisp
Sweet Fennel (a)	Spring	Seeds	3'–4' upright	Seeds, leaves—condiment. Aniselike flower stems eaten like celery	Seeds, leaves, stem	Poor	Full sun	Seeds, when ripe; leaves, as needed; stem, when tender
Tarragon (p)	Spring	Cuttings, division, plants	2' irregular	Seasoning	Leaves	Poor	Partial shade	As needed (fresh)
Thyme (p)	Fall or spring	Seeds, cuttings, division	6"–10" spreading	Seasoning	Leaves	Edging plant or among rocks	Full sun	Cut and dry leafy tops and flower clusters when first blooms open

*(a) = annual; (b) = biennial; (p) = perennial

Problems in Container Gardens

Container gardens are not without their problems. Most of the problems stem from inadequate light or improper watering and can be easily solved by minor adjustments. Plants are also susceptible to damage by certain destructive insects and plant diseases. These, too, can usually be controlled, either by washing the plant off or by applying an insecticide or a fungicide.

When troubles arise, act immediately to cure them, but do not overreact. Often enough, problems can be overcome simply by relocating a plant or by withholding water for a few days. This chapter is devoted to discussing the more common problems, their symptoms, and their cures.

Common Growth Problems

Yellowing of lower leaves. Newly purchased plants, shocked by a new environment, sometimes shed lower leaves. If leaf drop is accompanied by softening of the lower stems and a tendency of the soil to stay soggy, the problem may be too much water or poor drainage in the container. Withhold water for two or three days to see if the soil dries out. If it does not, repot the plant in a more porous soil mix, and fill the bottom of the container with pebbles to improve drainage. Overwatered cacti and succulents become mushy.

Wilting or curling of leaf edges. This could be caused by too little water, too much heat, too much fertilizer, too little humidity, or a combination of all of these. Damaged leaves may become brittle, develop brown spots, and fall off. Avoid placing plants near radiators or other heating outlets. If watering does not restore the plant to health, mist the foliage daily. Raise humidity by placing pots on a shallow tray of pebbles filled nearly to the top of the pebbles with water. Underwatered cacti and succulents may become pale or begin to yellow.

Brown or yellow spots on leaves. Such leaf markings are usually caused by too much light. Move the plant to a location where light is not as bright. If you are using artificial lighting, move the plants farther from the lights. If spots continue to develop, fungi may be the cause. Apply daconil or maneb according to label instructions.

Long, spindly stems and pale leaves. Plants tend to lean toward their source of light. If lighting is insufficient, the plants must "stretch," resulting in weak, spindly growth. Leaves may pale or appear stunted. Give afflicted plants a brighter location. If you are using artificial lighting, move the plants nearer the lamps. When normal growth resumes, pinch back leggy stems so that they are in proportion to the rest of the plant.

Tips of leaves turn brown. If leaves and stems are broken or bent, discoloration of the tips of the leaves may be the result of bruising. Ferns are particularly sensitive to bruising. Move plants to a location where they are less likely to be brushed against. Trim damaged parts with sharp scissors. Browning leaves can also indicate a pot-bound condition. Inspect roots to see if they are crowded and if so, repot the plant in a larger container.

Top leaves are stunted. If the plant produces rapid growth that never seems to mature, it may have received too much soluble fertilizer in one dose. Thus, the remainder of the fertilizer that the plant was unable to use drained through the soil, and the new growth is left with nothing to sustain it. Give the plant more light, and less fertilizer. Scrape off salts that have formed on the soil or the pots; then water thoroughly to leach out excess salts.

Leaves turn dull green to yellow, and bottom leaves drop. New leaves, if there are any at all, are stunted and weak. These are symptoms of nutrient deficiency. Fertilize plants more frequently, especially during the growing season.

Sudden dropping of leaves; leaves turn yellow. These symptoms are often caused by a sudden change in temperature. Some plants are especially sensitive to drafts and to temperature changes of as little as 5°. Plants exposed to the outdoors during winter, especially where winters are severe, may experience this sort of trauma. If the plant continues to lose leaves, check the roots to be certain they have not rotted. Be certain to keep plants away from radiators and out of drafts.

Seedlings die suddenly. Such seedlings may have been attacked by a fungus disease called "damping-off." Sterilize the potting soil and start again with fresh soil. (See "Soils and Growing Media" in Chapter One.) You may also want to buy seed that have been treated with a fungicide.

Pot-bound roots growing through drainage hole. Roots of overcrowded plants may also appear on the surface. Small and medium-size plants should be repotted when this occurs. If plants are too large to repot easily, loosen the surface soil, and remove the top 2 inches. Add fresh soil to replace what you have removed. This is called "top-dressing" the plant.

Knotted roots. If stunted growth causes you to suspect the plant needs repotting, and you discover that the roots are knotted and twisted, your problem may be nematodes. These microscopic creatures are often present in garden soil, and for this reason, potting soil should always be sterilized. Citrus and gardenia plants are highly susceptible to nematode problems.

Prune damaged roots and gently wash the old soil off the healthy roots. Repot the plant in sterilized potting soil and drench the soil with a nematocide, such as Nemagon or Fumazone. Sterilizing your potting soils will also help to avert fungus diseases.

If you must prune roots, remove a portion of the top growth as well to aid the roots in recovering. Root cuttings of top growth to propagate new plants in case nematode control on the mother plant is not possible.

Insect Pests

A number of insect pests may attack house plants. Always inspect plants carefully before buying to be certain the plants are free from insects and diseases. Plants that have been outside during the summer should be very closely inspected before they are brought back in. Cut flowers and other garden greenery used for indoor decoration may also harbor insects. Discard infested flower arrangements immediately; as pretty as the flowers may be, they are not worth the woes of trying to rid house plants of insect pests.

Should you discover infestation on a plant, segregate the plant immediately. Then inspect all your plants closely and segregate those with insects, no matter how minor the infestation may

appear; some insects reproduce with incredible speed.

If the infestation is light, sponge-bathe the foliage with a mild solution of household detergent and warm water (2 teaspoons detergent to 1 gallon water) to control insects. Smooth, broadleaf indoor plants, such as rubber plants, dieffenbachia, dracaena, and Chinese evergreen, should receive a regular monthly washing. Keep infested plants segregated and watch them closely for a few days to be certain the infestation is under control.

If the infestation is severe, it may be necessary to use insecticides to rid plants of insect pests. Most insecticides have offensive odors and should be applied outside or in a ventilated area such as a basement or garage. Spray both upper and lower leaf surfaces; most insects attack the lower surface first.

Hose down plants at least twice a month during the summer to prevent buildup of insects, especially during dry periods.

Glossary of Garden Terms

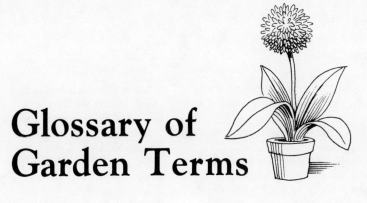

Air-borne fungi. Fungi that are transported by wind or other air movement.

Air-layering. A method of propagating (reproducing) plants by making a partial cut in the main stem of the plant on which roots then grow.

Annual. A plant that undergoes the entire life cycle of germination, growth, flower, and seed production in one season, then dies.

Axil. The crotch formed by the junction of leaf and branch or branch and trunk.

Biennial. A plant that undergoes its life cycle of germination, growth, flower, and seed production in two growing seasons, then dies.

Blight. A general term for fungus diseases which usually cause spotting and wilting of foliage.

Bonsai. The art of growing miniature trees. Plants may be dwarfed by nature or by the grower.

Bottle garden. A terrarium that uses a bottle as a container.

Bulb. An enlarged portion of root or subsurface stem in which plant nutrient is stored. The term bulb may also refer to a plant that has this type of root or stem.

Bulb fiber. A sphagnumlike material, usually of peat or osmunda, which is often used as a growing medium for potted bulbs.

Compost. Decomposed organic matter used in potting soil as a conditioner and mild fertilizer.

Crown. Top portion of root system where roots meet stem.

Culture. The cultivation of plants by man.

Cutting. A section of leaf, stem, or root used to start new plants. The cutting is placed in sand, peat moss, or other rooting media where it forms new roots.

Damping-off. A fungus disease that kills young seedling plants, usually without warning. May be averted by using sterilized soil.

Deciduous. Characterized by the loss of all of a plant's leaves during the dormant season.

Dish garden. A garden of miniature plants, usually planted in a dish, saucer, or other shallow, unenclosed container.

Division. The process of dividing the root system of a plant to form two or more new plants.

Dormant. Being at rest or in a period of non-growth. Many plants enter a dormant period during winter.

Double potting. Placing a potted plant in a larger pot with sphagnum moss or other moisture-retentive material between the walls of the two containers.

Epiphyte. An "air-borne" plant whose roots assimilate moisture and nutrients from the air and need no soil medium. Many bromeliads are epiphytes.

Fertilizer, liquid. A solution of water and soluble (dissolvable) fertilizer.

Fertilizer, slow-release. Any fertilizer that releases nutrients slowly to the plant.

Foliar watering. The practice of misting or spraying water on plant foliage.

Foot-candle. A measure of light; the amount of light cast by a candle on a surface 1 foot away.

Forcing bloom. Usually referring to bulbs and shrubs, the process of stimulating blooms out of season.

Fronds. The leaves of palms or ferns.

Fungicide. An agent, usually chemical, used to kill fungi.

Germination. The earliest stage of formation of a plant from seed, i.e., when the seed "sprouts."

Grafting. The practice of joining a branch or shoot of one plant to the stem or root system of another plant.

Gravel culture. A type of hydroponic culture in which gravel and water serve as the growing medium.

Hardening. Gradual acclimatization of a plant to any change of environment.

Hydroponics. A branch of plant cultivation in which water is used as the growing medium rather than soil.

Hygrometer. An instrument for measuring humidity or water vapor content of the atmosphere.

Insecticide. An agent, usually chemical, used for killing insects.

Jardiniere. A decorative container in which an already potted plant is placed.

Leaf mold. Partially decayed leaves.

Leggy. Characterized by long, spindly stems.

Loamy soil. A potting soil of equal parts loam, peat moss, and sand (or perlite).

Misting. Spraying leaves of a plant with water, a process also known as foliar feeding.

Mulch. Any material placed around the base of a plant to discourage weeds and conserve moisture. Common mulch materials include sawdust, pine straw, shredded bark, and compost among others.

Nematocide. An agent, usually chemical, for killing nematodes.

Nematode. Microscopic soil organism, many species of which are destructive to plants.

Offsets. Small plants that are produced at the base of a mature plant.

Opposite leaves. Leaves which grow opposite each other along a stem rather than alternately along the stem.

Organic matter. A general term for plant material at various stages of decomposition.

Peat moss. Partially decomposed sphagnum moss, used as a soil additive and valued particularly for its moisture-holding capacity: it can retain 6 to 10 times its weight in water.

Peaty soil. A soil mix containing 1 part loam, 1 part sand (or perlite), and 2 parts peat moss, leaf mold, or other decomposed organic matter.

Perennial. Usually referring to herbaceous plants that live for three years or more.

Perlite. A white granular material derived from silica; used as a substitute for sand in potting and rooting media.

Pesticide. An agent, usually chemical, for killing pests, such as insects, diseases, rodents, or weeds.

Pinching. Process of pinching off portions of stems to remove spindly growth and stimulate branching.

Planter. A large container, often stationary, for growing plants.

Plantlet. A small plant, often growing at the base of a mature plant, or at the end of an elongated stem, as in the case of the spider plant.

Plunging (pots). Burying pots in soil up to their rims; a recommended practice for plants that will be left unattended for a week or more.

Pot-bound. Severe constriction of plant roots in a container. Most pot-bound plants should be repotted.

Propagate. To stimulate plant reproduction. Common methods include seeds, cuttings, runners, offsets, and air-layering.

Pruning. The judicious removal of parts of a plant to encourage new growth, eliminate dead or diseased parts, or train to a desired form.

Raceme. An elongated main stem that bears flowers.

Repotting. Transferring a plant to a larger container when the plant becomes pot-bound or if destructive soil insects are detected.

Rooting. Stimulating root formation on a cutting taken from a plant.

Rooting medium. Any material in which roots may form on cuttings taken from a plant. Common rooting media include sand, perlite, peat moss, and sphagnum moss.

Runner. A plantlet borne by a mature plant on an elongated stem.

Sandy soil. A soil mix consisting of 1 part loam, 1 part peat moss or leaf mold, and 2 parts sand or perlite.

Sharp sand. Coarse sand, often called builder's sand.

Soil-borne fungi. Fungal organisms that live in the soil.

Sphagnum moss. Dried mosses found in bogs.

Stolon. A vinelike stem that grows along the ground or just under the surface and produces a new plant at its tip.

Subirrigating. Watering from the bottom of a container, usually done by placing a pot in a saucer or pan filled with water. Moisture is drawn up through the drainage hole in the bottom of the pot.

Succulent. A plant with thick, fleshy leaves and stems in which moisture is stored.

Sucker. A shoot that arises at the base of a mature plant.

Terrarium. An enclosed glass or plastic case in which plants are grown.

Topdressing. Removing the topmost soil from a large container and replacing it with fresh soil. This is a common practice with plants that are too large to repot. Excess root growth is also trimmed.

Tuber. A short, thickened, underground portion of stem or root from which the plant sends top growth.

Variegated foliage. Foliage characterized by an edging of white or yellow on leaf margins.

Vermiculite. A light, micalike material sometimes used as a rooting medium.

Water culture. See Hydroponics.

Index

95